GRILL COOKBOOK:

2 Books 1: A Complete Guide with Traditional Recipes for Beginners and Advanced. Smoke Dishes with SpecificInstructions, Cooking Temperature and Time

Mark Franklin

Table Of Contents

GRILL BEEF RECIPES

London Broil

Preparation Time: 20 minutes
Cooking Time: 12-16 minutes
Servings: 3-4
Ingredients:

- 1 (1½- to 2-pound) London broil or top round steak
- ¼ cup soy sauce
- 2 tablespoons white wine
- 2 tablespoons extra-virgin olive oil
- ¼ cup chopped scallions
- 2 tablespoons packed brown sugar
- 2 garlic cloves, minced
- 2 teaspoons red pepper flakes
- 1 teaspoon freshly ground black pepper

Directions:

1. Using a meat mallet, pound the steak lightly all over on both sides to break down its fibers and tenderize. You are not trying to pound down the thickness.
2. In a medium bowl, make the marinade by combining the soy sauce, white wine, olive oil, scallions, brown sugar, garlic, red pepper flakes, and black pepper.
3. Put the steak in a shallow plastic container with a lid and pour the marinade over the meat. Cover and refrigerate for 4 hours.
4. Supply your smoker with wood pellets and follow the manufacturer's specific start-up procedure. Preheat, with the lid closed, to 350°F.
5. Place the steak directly on the grill, close the lid, and smoke for 6 minutes. Flip, then smoke with the lid closed for 6 to 10 minutes more, or until a meat thermometer inserted in the meat reads 130°F for medium-rare.
6. The meat's temperature will rise by about 5 degrees while it rests.

Nutrition: Calories: 316 Cal Fat: 3 g Carbohydrates: 0 g Protein: 54 g Fiber: 0 g

French Onion Burgers

Preparation Time: 35 minutes
Cooking Time: 20-25 minutes
Servings: 4
Ingredients:

- 1-pound lean ground beef
- 1 tablespoon minced garlic
- 1 teaspoon Better Than Bouillon Beef Base
- 1 teaspoon dried chives
- 1 teaspoon freshly ground black pepper
- 8 slices Gruyere cheese, divided
- ½ cup soy sauce
- 1 tablespoon extra-virgin olive oil
- 1 teaspoon liquid smoke
- 3 medium onions, cut into thick slices (do not separate the rings)
- 1 loaf French bread, cut into 8 slices
- 4 slices provolone cheese

Directions:

1. In a large bowl, mix together the ground beef, minced garlic, beef base, chives, and pepper until well blended.
2. Divide the meat mixture and shape into 8 thin burger patties.
3. Top each of 4 patties with one slice of Gruyere, then top with the remaining 4 patties to create 4 stuffed burgers.
4. Supply your smoker with wood pellets and follow the manufacturer's specific start-up procedure. Preheat, with the lid closed, to 425°F.
5. Arrange the burgers directly on one side of the grill, close the lid, and smoke for 10 minutes. Flip and smoke with the lid closed for 10 to 15 minutes more, or until a meat thermometer inserted in the burgers reads 160°F. Add another Gruyère slice to the burgers during the last 5 minutes of smoking to melt.
6. Meanwhile, in a small bowl, combine the soy sauce, olive oil, and liquid smoke.
7. Arrange the onion slices on the grill and paste on both sides with the soy sauce mixture. Smoke with the lid closed for 20 minutes, flipping halfway through.
8. Lightly toast the French bread slices on the grill. Layer each of 4 slices with a burger patty, a slice of provolone cheese, and some of the smoked onions. Top each with another slice of toasted French bread. Serve immediately.

Nutrition: Calories: 704 Cal Fat: 43 g Carbohydrates: 28 g Protein: 49 g Fiber: 2 g

Beef Shoulder Clod

Preparation Time: 10 minutes
Cooking Time: 12-16 hours
Servings: 16-20
Ingredients:

- ½ cup sea salt
- ½ cup freshly ground black pepper
- 1 tablespoon red pepper flakes
- 1 tablespoon minced garlic
- 1 tablespoon cayenne pepper
- 1 tablespoon smoked paprika
- 1 (13- to 15-pound) beef shoulder clod

Directions:

1. Combine spices
2. Generously apply it to the beef shoulder.
3. Supply your smoker with wood pellets and follow the manufacturer's specific start-up procedure. Preheat, with the lid closed, to 250°F.
4. Put the meat on the grill grate, close the lid, and smoke for 12 to 16 hours, or until a meat thermometer inserted deeply into the beef reads 195°F. You may need to cover the clod with aluminum foil toward the end of smoking to prevent overbrowning.
5. Let the meat rest and serve

Nutrition: Calories: 290 Cal Fat: 22 g Carbohydrates: 0 g Protein: 20 g Fiber: 0 g

Corned Beef and Cabbage

Preparation Time: 30 minutes
Cooking Time: 4-5 hours
Servings: 6-8
Ingredients:

- 1-gallon water
- 1 (3- to 4-pound) point cut corned beef brisket with pickling spice packet
- 1 tablespoon freshly ground black pepper
- 1 tablespoon garlic powder
- ½ cup molasses
- 1 teaspoon ground mustard
- 1 head green cabbage
- 4 tablespoons (½ stick) butter
- 2 tablespoons rendered bacon fat
- 1 chicken bouillon cube, crushed

Directions:

1. Refrigerate overnight, changing the water as often as you remember to do so—ideally, every 3 hours while you're awake—to soak out some of the curing salt initially added.
2. Supply your smoker with wood pellets and follow the manufacturer's specific start-up procedure. Preheat, with the lid closed, to 275°F.
3. Remove the meat from the brining liquid, pat it dry, and generously rub with the black pepper and garlic powder.
4. Put the seasoned corned beef directly on the grill, fat-side up, close the lid, and grill for 2 hours. Remove from the grill when done.
5. In a small bowl, combine the molasses and ground mustard and pour half of this mixture into the bottom of a disposable aluminum pan.
6. Transfer the meat to the pan, fat-side up, and pour the remaining molasses mixture on top, spreading it evenly over the meat. Cover tightly with aluminum foil.
7. Transfer the pan to the grill, close the lid, and continue smoking the corned beef for 2 to 3 hours, or until a meat thermometer inserted in the thickest part reads 185°F.
8. Rest meat
9. Serve.

Nutrition: Calories: 295 Cal Fat: 17 g Carbohydrates: 19 g Protein: 18 g Fiber: 6 g

Cheeseburger Hand Pies

Preparation Time: 35 minutes
Cooking Time: 10 minutes
Servings: 6
Ingredients:

- ½ pound lean ground beef
- 1 tablespoon minced onion
- 1 tablespoon steak seasoning
- 1 cup cheese
- 8 slices white American cheese, divided
- 2 (14-ounce) refrigerated prepared pizza dough sheets, divided
- 2 eggs
- 24 hamburger dill pickle chips
- 2 tablespoons sesame seeds
- 6 slices tomato, for garnish
- Ketchup and mustard, for serving

Directions:

1. Supply your smoker with wood pellets and follow the manufacturer's specific start-up procedure. Preheat, with the lid closed, to 325°F.
2. On your stove top, in a medium sauté pan over medium-high heat, brown the ground beef for 4 to 5 minutes, or until cooked through. Add the minced onion and steak seasoning.
3. Toss in the shredded cheese blend and 2 slices of American cheese and stir until melted and fully incorporated.
4. Remove the cheeseburger mixture from the heat and set aside.
5. Make sure the dough is well chilled for easier handling. Working quickly, roll out one prepared pizza crust on parchment paper and brush with half of the egg wash.
6. Arrange the remaining 6 slices of American cheese on the dough to outline 6 hand pies.

Nutrition: Calories: 325 Cal Fat: 21 g Carbohydrates: 11 g Protein: 23 g Fiber: 0 g

Pastrami

Preparation Time: 10 minutes
Cooking Time: 4-5 hours
Servings: 12
Ingredients:

- 1-gallon water, plus ½ cup
- ½ cup packed light brown sugar
- 1 (3- to 4-pound) point cut corned beef brisket with brine mix packet
- 2 tablespoons freshly ground black pepper
- ¼ cup ground coriander

Directions:

1. Cover and refrigerate overnight, changing the water as often as you remember to do so—ideally, every 3 hours while you're awake—to soak out some of the curing salt originally added.
2. Supply your smoker with wood pellets and follow the manufacturer's specific start-up procedure. Preheat, with the lid closed, to 275°F.
3. In a small bowl, combine the black pepper and ground coriander to form a rub.
4. Drain the meat, pat it dry, and generously coat on all sides with the rub.
5. Place the corned beef directly on the grill, fat-side up, close the lid, and smoke for 3 hours to 3 hours 30 minutes, or until a meat thermometer inserted in the thickest part reads 175°F to 185°F.
6. Add the corned beef, cover tightly with aluminum foil, and smoke on the grill with the lid closed for an additional 30 minutes to 1 hour.
7. Remove the meat
8. Refrigerate

Nutrition: Calories: 123 Cal Fat: 4 g Carbohydrates: 3 g Protein: 16 g Fiber: 0 g

Smoked and Pulled Beef

Preparation Time: 10 Minutes
Cooking Time: 6 Hours
Servings: 6
Ingredients:

- 4 lb. beef sirloin tip roast
- 1/2 cup BBQ rub
- Two bottles of amber beer
- One bottle barbecues sauce

Directions:

1. Turn your wood pellet grill onto smoke setting, then trim excess fat from the steak.
2. Coat the steak with BBQ rub and let it smoke on the grill for 1 hour.
3. Continue cooking and flipping the steak for the next 3 hours. Transfer the steak to a braising vessel. Add the beers.
4. Braise the beef until tender, then transfer to a platter reserving 2 cups of cooking liquid.
5. Use a pair of forks to shred the beef and return it to the pan. Add the reserved liquid and barbecue sauce. Stir well and keep warm before serving.
6. Enjoy.

Nutrition: Calories 829 Total fat 46g Total carbs 4g Protein 86g Sodium: 181mg

GRILL PORK RECIPES

Pork Jerky

Preparation Time: 15 minutes

Cook time: 2 hours 30 minutes

Servings: 12

Ingredients:

- 4 pounds' boneless center-cut pork (trimmed of excess fat and sliced into ¼ inch thick slices)

Marinade:

- 1/3 cup soy sauce
- 1 cup pineapple juice
- 1 tbsp. rice wine vinegar
- 2 tsp black pepper
- 1 tsp red pepper flakes
- 5 tbsp. brown sugar
- 1 tsp paprika
- 1 tsp onion powder
- 1 tsp garlic powder
- 2 tsp salt or to taste

Directions:

1. Combine and mix all the marinade ingredients in a mixing bowl.
2. Put the sliced pork in a gallon-sized zip-lock bag and pour the marinade into the bag. Massage the marinade into the pork. Seal the bag and refrigerate for 8 hours.
3. Activate the pellet grill smoker setting and leave the lip open for 5 minutes until the fire starts.
4. Close the lid and preheat your pellet grill to 180°F, using a hickory pellet.
5. Remove the pork slices from the marinade and pat them dry with a paper towel.
6. Arrange the pork slices on the grill in a single layer. Smoke the pork for about 2 ½ hours, often turning after the first 1 hour of smoking. The jerky should be dark and dry when it is done.

7. Remove the jerky from the grill and let it sit for about 1 hour to cool.
8. Serve immediately or store in airtight containers and refrigerate for future use.

Nutrition: Calories: 260 Fat: 11.4g Cholesterol: 80mg Carbohydrate: 8.6g Protein: 28.1g

Grilled Carnitas

Preparation Time: 20 minutes
Cook time: 10 hours
Servings: 12
Ingredients:

- 1 tsp paprika
- 1 tsp oregano
- 1 tsp cayenne pepper
- 2 tsp brown sugar
- 1 tsp mint
- 1 tbsp. onion powder
- 1 tsp cumin
- 1 tsp chili powder
- 2 tbsp. salt
- 1 tsp garlic powder
- 1 tsp Italian seasoning
- 2 tbsp. Olive oil.
- 5 pounds' pork shoulder roast

Directions:

1. Trim the pork of any excess fat.
2. To make a rub, combine the paprika, oregano, cayenne, sugar, mint, onion powder, garlic powder, cumin, chili, salt, and Italian seasoning in a small mixing bowl.
3. Rub all sides of the pork with the rub.
4. Start your grill for smoking, leaving the lid open until the fire starts.
5. Close the lid and preheat the grill to 325°F with the lid closed for 15 minutes.
6. Place the pork in a foil pan and place the pan on the grill—Cook for about 2 hours.
7. After 2 hours, increase the heat to 325°F and smoke pork for an additional 8 hours or until the pork's internal temperature reaches 190°F.
8. Remove pork from it and let it sit until it is cook and easy to handle.
9. Shred the pork with two forks.
10. Place a cast-iron skillet on the grill grate and add the olive oil.
11. Add the pork and sear until the pork is brown and crispy.
12. Remove pork from heat and let it rest for a few minutes. Serve!

Nutrition: Calories: 514 Fat: 41.1g Cholesterol: 134mg Carbohydrate: 1.6g Protein: 32g

Stuffed Tenderloin

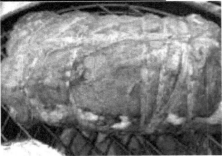

Preparation Time: 15 minutes

Cook time: 3 hours
Servings: 8
Ingredients:
- 1 pork tenderloin
- 12 slices of bacon
- ¼ cup cheddar cheese
- ¼ cup mozzarella cheese
- 1 small onion (finely chopped)
- 1 carrot (finely chopped)

Rub:

- ½ tsp granulated garlic (not garlic powder)
- ½ tsp cayenne pepper
- 1 tsp paprika
- ½ tsp ground pepper
- 1 tsp chili
- ½ tsp onion powder
- ¼ tsp cumin
- 1 tsp salt

Directions:

1. Butterfly the pork tenderloin and place between 2 plastic wraps. Pound the tenderloin evenly with a mallet until it is ½ inch thick.
2. Place the cheddar, mozzarella, onion, and carrot on one end of the flat pork. Roll up the pork like a burrito.
3. Combine all the ingredients for the rub in a mixing bowl. Rub the seasoning mixture all over the pork.
4. Wrap the pork with bacon slices.
5. Preheat the grill to 275°F for 10-15 minutes. Use apple, hickory, or mesquite hard pellets.
6. Place the pork on the grill and smoke for 3 hours, or until the pork's internal temperature reaches 165°F and the bacon wrap is crispy.

7. Remove the pork from heat and let it rest for about 10 minutes.
8. Cut into sizes and serve.

Nutrition: Calories: 241 Fat: 14.8g Cholesterol: 66mg Carbohydrate: 2.7g Protein: 22.9g

Maplewood Bourbon BBQ Ham

Preparation Time: 15 minutes
Cook time: 2 hours 30 minutes
Servings: 8
Ingredients:

- 1 large ham
- 1/2 cup brown sugar
- 3 tbsp. bourbon
- 2 tbsp. lemon
- 2 tbsp. Dijon mustard
- ¼ cup apple juice
- ¼ cup maple syrup
- 1 tsp salt
- 1 tsp freshly ground garlic
- 1 tsp ground black pepper

Directions:

1. Start your grill on a smoke setting, leaving for 5 minutes, until the fire starts.
2. Close the lid and preheat the grill to 325°F.
3. Place the ham on a smoker rack and place the rack on the grill. Smoke for 2 hours or until the internal temperature of the ham reaches 125°F.
4. Combine the sugar, bourbon, lemon, mustard, apple juice, salt, pepper, and maple in a saucepan over medium to high heat.
5. Bring mixture to a boil, reduce the heat and simmer until the sauce thickens.
6. Glaze the ham with maple mixture.
7. Increase the grill temperature to 375°F and continue cooking until the internal temperature of the ham reaches 140°F.
8. Remove the glazed ham from the grill and let it rest for about 15 minutes.
9. Cut ham into small sizes and serve.

Nutrition: Calories: 163 Fat: 4.6g Cholesterol: 29mg Carbohydrate: 19g Protein: 8.7g

Pork Steak

Preparation Time: 10 minutes
Cooking Time: 20 minutes
Servings: 4
Ingredients:

For the Brine:

- 2-inch piece of orange peel
- 2 sprigs of thyme
- 4 tablespoons salt
- 4 black peppercorns
- 1 sprig of rosemary
- 2 tablespoons brown sugar
- 2 bay leaves
- 10 cups water

For Pork Steaks:

- 4 pork steaks, fat trimmed
- Game rub as needed

Directions:

1. Prepare the brine and for this, take a large container, place all of its ingredients in it and stir until sugar has dissolved.
2. Place steaks in it, add some weights to keep steak submerge into the brine, and let soak for 24 hours in the refrigerator.
3. Fill the grill hopper with hickory flavored pellets, power the grill on by using the control panel, select 'smoke' on the temperature dial, or set the temperature to 225°F and let it preheat for a minimum of 15 minutes.
4. Remove steaks from the brine, rinse well, and pat dry with paper towels and then season well with game rub until coated.
5. When the grill has preheated, open the lid, place steaks on the grill grate, shut the grill, and smoke for 10 minutes per side until the internal temperature reaches 140°F.
6. Transfer steaks to a cutting board, rest for 10 minutes, and then cut into slices and serve.

Nutrition: Calories: 260 Fat: 21g Carbs: 1g Protein: 17g

Carolina Smoked Ribs

Preparation Time: 30 minutes

Cooking Time: 4 hours 30 minutes

Serving: 10

Ingredients:

- 1/2 a cup of brown sugar
- 1/3 cup of fresh lemon juice
- ¼ cup of white vinegar
- 1/4 cup of apple cider vinegar
- 1 tablespoon of Worcestershire sauce
- ¼ cup of molasses
- 2 cups of prepared mustard
- 2 teaspoons of garlic, minced
- 2 teaspoons of salt
- 1 teaspoon of ground black pepper
- 1 teaspoon of crushed red pepper flakes
- ½ a teaspoon of white pepper
- ¼ teaspoon of cayenne pepper
- 2 racks of pork spare ribs
- ½ a cup of barbeque seasoning

Directions:

1. Take a medium-sized bowl and whisk in brown sugar, white vinegar, lemon juice, mustard, Worcestershire sauce, mustard, molasses
2. Mix well and season the mixture with granulated garlic, pepper, salt, red pepper flakes, white pepper flakes, cayenne pepper
3. Take your drip pan and add water; cover with aluminum foil. Pre-heat your smoker to 225 degrees F
4. Use water fill water pan halfway through and place it over drip pan. Add wood chips to the side tray
5. Rub the ribs with your prepared seasoning and transfer to your smoker
6. Cover the meat with aluminum foil and smoke for 4 hours, making sure to add chips after every 60 minutes
7. After the first 3 and a ½ hours, make sure to uncover the meat and baste it generously with the prepared mustard sauce
8. Take the meat out and serve with remaining sauce
9. Enjoy!

Nutrition: Calories: 750 Fat: 50g Carbohydrates: 24g Fiber: 2.2g

Hearty Pig Candies

Preparation Time: 20 minutes
Cooking Time: 2 hours
Servings: 10
Ingredients:

- Nonstick cooking spray
- 2 pound of bacon slices
- 1 cup of firmly packed brown sugar
- 2-3 teaspoon of cayenne pepper
- ½ a cup of maple syrup

Directions:

1. Take your drip pan and add water; cover with aluminum foil. Pre-heat your smoker to 225 degrees F
2. Use water fill water pan halfway through and place it over drip pan. Add wood chips to the side tray
3. Remove the grill rack from your smoker and cover with aluminum foil; spray the foils with cooking spay
4. Lay the bacon in a single layer, making sure to leave a bit of space in between
5. Take a small bowl and add brown sugar, cayenne, and mix
6. Baste the bacon with ¼ cup of maple syrup
7. Sprinkle half of the rub on top of the bacon
8. Transfer the rack to the smoker alongside the bacon and smoke for 1 hour
9. Flip the bacon and baste with another ¼ cup of maple syrup, sprinkle more rub, and a smoker for 1 hour more
10. Once the bacon is brown and firm, it's ready to be served!

Nutrition: Calories: 152 Fats: 10g Carbs: 13g Fiber: 2g

Sauced Up Pork Spares

Preparation Time: 5 hours
Cooking Time: 4 hours
Serving: 6
Ingredients:

- 6 pound of pork spareribs

For Dry Rub

- ½ a cup of packed brown sugar
- 2 tablespoons of chili powder
- 1 tablespoon of paprika
- 1 tablespoon of freshly ground black pepper
- 2 tablespoons of garlic powder
- 2 teaspoons of onion powder
- 2 teaspoons of kosher salt
- 2 teaspoons of ground cumin
- 1 teaspoon of ground cinnamon
- 1 teaspoon of jalapeno seasoning salt
- 1 teaspoon of Cayenne pepper

For Mop Sauce

- 1 cup of apple cider
- ¾ cup of apple cider vinegar
- 1 tablespoon of onion powder
- 1 tablespoon of garlic powder
- 2 tablespoon of lemon juice
- 1 jalapeno pepper, chopped
- 3 tablespoon of hot pepper sauce
- Kosher salt as needed
- Black pepper as needed
- 2 cups of soaked wood chips

Directions:

1. Take a medium-sized bowl and add brown sugar, chili powder, 2 tablespoons of garlic powder, 2 teaspoons of onion powder, cumin, cinnamon, kosher salt, cayenne pepper, jalapeno seasoning Mix well and rub the mixture over the pork spare ribs
2. Allow it to refrigerate for 4 hours
3. Take your drip pan and add water; cover with aluminum foil. Pre-heat your smoker to 225 degrees F Use water fill water pan halfway through and place it over drip pan. Add wood chips to the side tray Take a medium bowl and stir in apple cider, apple cider vinegar, 1 tablespoon of onion powder, jalapeno, 1 tablespoon of garlic powder, salt, pepper, and lemon juice
4. Add a handful of soaked wood chips and transfer the ribs to your smoker middle rack
5. Smoke for 3-4 hours, making sure to keep adding chips after every hour
6. Take the meat out and serve!

Nutrition: Calories: 1591 Fats: 120g Carbs: 44g Fiber: 3g

Porky Onion Soup

Preparation Time: 2 hours

Cooking Time: 4 hours 30 minutes

Serving: 6

Ingredients:

- 1 full rack of pork spare ribs
- 2 packs onion soup mix of your choice
- BBQ Pork Rub
- 4 cups of water

Directions:

1. Remove the white membrane of the pork meat and trim off any excess fat
2. Take your drip pan and add water; cover with aluminum foil. Pre-heat your smoker to 225 degrees F
3. Use water fill water pan halfway through and place it over drip pan. Add wood chips to the side tray
4. Prepare your rub mixture by mixing salt, garlic powder, pepper, and paprika in a bowl
5. Rub the rib with the mixture
6. Transfer to the smoker and smoker for 2 hours
7. Blend 2 packs of onion soup with 4 cups of water
8. Once smoking is complete, take a heavy aluminum foil and transfer the meat to the foil, pour the soup mix all over
9. Seal the ribs
10. Smoke for another 1 and a ½ hours
11. Gently open the foil and turn the rib, seal it up and smoke for 1 hour more
12. Slice and serve!

Nutrition: Calories: 461 Fats: 22g Carbs: 17g Fiber: 4g

Lovely Pork Butt

Preparation Time: 2 hours + 4 hours soak time

Cooking Time: 20 minutes

Servings: 18

Ingredients:

- 7 pounds' fresh pork butt roast
- 2 tablespoons ground Mexico Chile Powder
- 4 tablespoons brown sugar, packed

Directions:

1. Start by soaking up your Pork Butt in a finely prepared brine (salt) solution for 4 hours at least and overnight at max
2. Make sure to cover the Butt up before placing it in your fridge
3. Take your drip pan and add water; cover with aluminum foil. Pre-heat your smoker to 225 degrees F
4. Use water fill water pan halfway through and place it over drip pan. Add wood chips to the side tray
5. Take a small-sized bowl and toss in the chili powder, brown sugar alongside any other seasoning which you may fancy
6. Rub the butt with your prepared mixture finely
7. Finely take a roasting rack and place it in a drip pan
8. Lay your butt on top of the rack
9. Smoke the butt for about 6-18 hours (Keep in mind that the pork will be done once the temperature of its internals reaches 100-degree Fahrenheit)
10. Serve hot

Nutrition: Calories: 326 Fats: 21g Carbs:4g Fiber: 0.5g

Strawberry and Jalapeno Smoked Ribs

Preparation Time: 15 minutes
Cooking Time: 90 minutes
Serving: 8
Ingredients:

- 3 tablespoons of Kosher Salt
- 2 tablespoons of Ground Cumin
- 1 tablespoon of Dried Oregano
- 1 tablespoon of garlic, minced
- 2 teaspoons of chili powder
- 1 teaspoon of ground black pepper
- 1 teaspoon of celery seed
- 1 teaspoon of dried thyme
- 1 rack of spareribs
- 2 slabs of baby back pork ribs
- 1 cup of apple juice
- 2 jalapeno peppers. cut half in lengthwise and deseeded
- ½ a mug of beer
- ½ onion, chopped
- ¼ cup of sugar-free strawberry
- 3 tablespoon of BBQ sauce
- 1 tablespoon of olive oil
- 2 cloves of garlic
- Sea salt as needed
- Ground pepper as needed

Directions:

1. Take a bowl first and blend in your salt, oregano, cumin, minced garlic, 1 teaspoon of ground black pepper, chili powder, ground thyme, and celery seed ad toss them in a food processor
2. Place your baby back rib slabs and spare rib rack on sheets of aluminum foil and rub the spice mix all over their body
3. Fold up the foil around each of them
4. Divide and pour the apple juice amongst the foil packets and foil the edges together to seal them up
5. Let them marinate for about 8 hours or overnight
6. Prepare your oven rack and place it about 6 inches away from the heat source, and pre-heat your ove3n's broiler
7. Line up a baking sheet with the aluminum foil and place your jalapeno pepper on top of it, with the cut upsides down
8. Cook Jalapeno peppers for 8 minutes under the broiler until the skin is blackened
9. Toss them and seal it up using a plastic wrap
10. Let the peppers steam off for 20 minutes
11. Remove them and discard the skin

12. Blend the jalapeno peppers, onion, beer, strawberry preserve, olive oil, BBQ sauce, sea salt, and just a pinch of ground black pepper altogether in a blender until the sauce is fully smoothened out
13. Transfer the sauce to a container and let cover it up with a lid; let it chill for 8 hours or overnight
14. Take your drip pan and add water; cover with aluminum foil. Pre-heat your smoker to 225 degrees F
15. Use water fill water pan halfway through and place it over drip pan. Add wood chips to the side tray
16. Smoke for 60 minutes
17. Increase the temp to 225 degrees Fahrenheit or 110 degrees Celsius and keep cooking for another 2-3 hours
18. Preheat your smoker to a temperature of 250 degrees Fahrenheit or 120 degrees Celsius
19. Unwrap your cooked ribs and toss away the apple juice
20. Place them on top of your smoker
21. Cook on your smoker until the surface of your meat is finely dried up; it should take about 5-10 minutes
22. After which, continue cooking, making sure to brush it up with the sauce after every 15 minutes
23. Turn it around after 30 minutes
24. Repeat and cook for 1 hour
25. Serve hot when tender

Nutrition: Fats: 41.2g Carbs: 8.2g Fiber: 0.7g

GRILL LAMB RECIPES

Grilled Rosemary Lamb with Juicy Tomatoes

Preparation Time: 10 Minutes
Cooking Time: 40 Minutes
Servings: 6

Ingredients

- Lamb and Sauce
- 1 3–4lb of boneless lamb shoulder
- Kosher salt and grounded pepper
- Two chopped red onions
- One bunch of rosemary leaves
- One bunch of oregano leaves
- ¾ cup of red wine vinegar
- ¼ cup of extra virgin olive oil
- 1 cup plain whole-milk Greek yogurt
- ¼ cup of fresh lemon juice
- One grated garlic clove
- Tomatoes and Assembly
- Five beefsteak tomatoes (about 4 lb.)
- sea salt flakes grounded black pepper
- 3 tbsp. of fresh lemon juice
- One halved red onion, thinly sliced
- extra virgin olive oil

Directions:

Lamb and Sauce

1. Put the lamb shoulder, cut side up, on a slicing board. Use a sharp knife to separate the beef into smaller portions along its herbal seams. You should discover yourself with five or 1/2 dozen pieces of assorted sizes. Put the lamb into a tumbler baking dish and season with salt and grounded pepper.
2. Mix the onions, rosemary leaves, and oregano leaves till finely chopped. Add the vinegar and the oil and blend till rigid purée forms. Season the marinade with salt and pepper, and then pour it over the lamb pieces. Cover and allow it to take a seat for two or three hours.
3. Mix the yogurt, the lemon juice, and garlic in a medium bowl. Put some seasonings in the sauce with salt and pepper, then cowl and relax.
4. Do Ahead: Lamb may be seasoned one day in advance and the sauce-eight hours ahead.

Tomatoes and Assembly

1. Before grilling, slice the tomatoes into ½"thick rounds and put them onto a platter. Season with salt and black pepper, then drizzle with 1/2 of the lemon juice. Add onion, season with salt and pepper, drizzle the ultimate juice over, unfold rosemary sprigs, and then be placed apart.
2. Set up the grill for medium warmness. Put the larger lamb pieces onto the grate and grill till the lowest is well brown, about five minutes. Spoon some remaining marinade

over the lamb, flip and keep grilling, turning every five minutes until the lamb is roasted in spots and well browned.

3. After a quarter-hour greater or much less, upload the smaller pieces to the grill and comply with the same instructions. They take less time to cook. The instant-read thermometer inserted into the middle of every part must register a hundred and forty for large portions. Begin checking the smaller ones after 7 to 10 minutes. As every bit finishes, circulate onto a platter, spreading on the rosemary. Let it rest for at least 20 or 30 minutes.

4. Move the lamb onto a reducing board and add rosemary sprigs on the perimeters of the platter. Tip the platter just so gathered tomato and lamb juices pool at one cease and spoon over the tomatoes. With a pointy knife, slice the lamb into skinny portions and add onion and tomatoes: season with salt and drizzle with oil.

5. Sprinkle with the yogurt sauce and additional virgin oil and serve.

Nutrition: Energy (calories): 311 kcal Protein: 36.21 g Fat: 15.73 g Carbohydrates: 5.88 g

Smoked Lamb Chops (Lollipops)

Preparation Time: 20 Minutes
Cooking Time: 55 Minutes
Servings: 4 Persons

Ingredients

- 2 tbsp. fresh sage
- One rack of lamb
- Two garlic cloves, large, roughly chopped
- 1 tbsp. fresh thyme
- Three sprigs of fresh rosemary, approximately 2 tbsps.
- ¼ cup olive oil
- 2 tbsp. shallots, roughly chopped
- 1 tbsp. honey
- ½ teaspoon each of course ground pepper & salt

Directions

1. Using a fruitwood, preheat your smoker to 225 F in advance.
2. Trim any silver pores and skin & excess fats from the rack of lamb.
3. Thoroughly combine the leftover ingredients collectively (for the herb paste) in a food processor & liberally practice the paste over the rack of lamb.
4. Place the covered lamb at the preheated smoker & cook until the rack of lamb's internal temperature displays 120 F, for 45 minutes to 55 minutes. Remove the beef & prepare your smoker or grill for direct warmness now.
5. Cook until brown the lamb for a few minutes on every side. Let rest for five minutes, after which, slice into person lollipops; serve warm & enjoy.

Nutrition: 184 Calories 16g Total Fat 12mg of Cholesterol 75mg of Potassium 6g Total Carbohydrates 4.2g Protein

Blackstone Garlic Rack Lamb

Preparation Time: 45 Minutes
Cooking Time: 3 Hours
Servings: 4
Ingredients:

- Lamb Rack
- Basil – 1 teaspoon
- Oregano – 1 teaspoon
- Peppermill – 10 cranks
- Marsala wine – 3 oz.
- Cram Sherry – 3 oz.
- Olive oil
- Madeira wine – 3 oz
- Balsamic vinegar – 3 oz.
- Rosemary – 1 teaspoon

Directions:

1. Add all of the ingredients into a zip bag the mix well to form an emulsion.
2. Place the rack lamb into the bag the release all of the air as you rub the marinade all over the lamb.
3. Let it stay in the bag for about 45 minutes
4. Get the wood pellet grill preheated to 2500F, then cook the lamb for 3 hours as you turn on both sides.
5. Ensure that the internal temperature is at 1650F before removing from the grill.
6. Allow to cool for a few minutes, then serve and enjoy.

Nutrition: Calories: 291 Cal Protein: 26 g Fat: 21 g

Blackstone Braised Lamb Shank

Preparation Time: 20 Minutes
Cooking Time: 4 Hours
Servings: 6
Ingredients:

- Lamb shanks – 4
- Olive oil as required
- Beef broth – 1 cup
- Red wine – 1 cup
- Fresh thyme and sprigs – 4

Directions:

1. Season lamb shanks with prime rib rub, then allow resting.
2. Get the wood pellet grill temperature set to high, then cook the lamb shanks for about 30 minutes.
3. Place the shanks directly on the grill grate, then cook for another 20 minutes until browned on the outside.
4. Transfer the cooked lamb shanks into a Dutch oven, then pour beef broth, the herbs, and wine. Cover it with a fitting lid, then place it back on the grill grate and allow it to cook at a reduced temperature of 3250F.
5. Brace the lamb shanks for about 3 hours or until the internal temperature gets to 1800F.
6. Remove the lid once ready, then serve on a platter together with the accumulated juices and enjoy.

Nutrition: Calories: 312 Cal Protein: 27 g Fat: 24 g

GRILL POULTRY RECIPES

Wood Pellet Grilled Chicken Kabobs

Preparation Time: 45 minutes
Cooking Time: 12 minutes
Servings: 6
Ingredients:

- 1/2 cup olive oil
- 2 tbsp white vinegar
- 1 tbsp lemon juice
- 1-1/2 tbsp salt
- 1/2 tbsp pepper, coarsely ground
- 2 tbsp chives, freshly chopped
- 1-1/2 tbsp thyme, freshly chopped
- 2 tbsp Italian parsley freshly chopped
- 1tbsp garlic, minced
- Kabobs
- 1 each orange, red, and yellow pepper
- 1-1/2 pounds chicken breast, boneless and skinless
- 12 mini mushrooms

Directions:

1. In a mixing bowl, add all the marinade ingredients and mix well. Toss the chicken and mushrooms in the marinade then refrigerate for 30 minutes.
2. Meanwhile, soak the skewers in hot water. Remove the chicken from the fridge and start assembling the kabobs.
3. Preheat your wood pellet to 450°F.
4. Grill the kabobs in the wood pellet for 6 minutes, flip them and grill for 6 more minutes.
5. Remove from the grill and let rest. Heat up the naan bread on the grill for 2 minutes.
6. Serve and enjoy.

Nutrition: Calories: 165 Cal Fat: 13 g Carbohydrates: 1 g Protein: 33 g Fiber: 0 g

Wood Pellet Grilled Chicken

Preparation Time: 10 minutes
Cooking Time: 1 hour and 10 minutes
Servings: 6
Ingredients:

- 5 pounds whole chicken
- 1/2 cup oil
- Chicken rub

Directions:

1. Preheat your wood pellet on smoke with the lid open for 5 minutes. Close the lid, increase the temperature to 450°F and preheat for 15 more minutes.
2. Tie the chicken legs together with the baker's twine then rub the chicken with oil and coat with chicken rub.
3. Place the chicken on the grill with the breast side up.
4. Grill the chicken for 70 minutes without opening it or until the internal temperature reaches 165°F.
5. Once the chicken is out of the grill let it cool down for 15 minutes
6. Enjoy.

Nutrition: Calories: 935 Cal Fat: 53 g Carbohydrates: 0 g Protein: 107 g Fiber: 0 g

Wood Pellet Chicken Breasts

Preparation Time: 10 minutes
Cooking Time: 15 minutes
Servings: 6
Ingredients:

- 3 chicken breasts
- 1 tbsp avocado oil
- 1/4 tbsp garlic powder
- 1/4 tbsp onion powder
- 3/4 tbsp salt
- 1/4 tbsp pepper

Directions:

1. Preheat your pellet to 375°F.
2. Half the chicken breasts lengthwise then coat with avocado oil.
3. With the spices, drizzle it on all sides to season
4. Drizzle spices to season the chicken
5. Put the chicken on top of the grill and begin to cook until its internal temperature approaches 165 degrees Fahrenheit
6. Put the chicken on top of the grill and begin to cook until it rises to a temperature of 165 degrees Fahrenheit
7. Serve and enjoy.

Nutrition: Calories: 120 Cal Fat: 4 g Carbohydrates: 0 g Protein: 19 g Fiber: 0 g

Wood Pellet Smoked Spatchcock Turkey

Preparation Time: 30 minutes
Cooking Time: 1 hour and 45 minutes
Servings: 6
Ingredients:

- 1 whole turkey
- 1/2 cup oil
- 1/4 cup chicken rub
- 1 tbsp onion powder
- 1 tbsp garlic powder
- 1 tbsp rubbed sage

Directions:

1. Preheat your wood pellet grill to high.
2. Meanwhile, place the turkey on a platter with the breast side down then cut on either side of the backbone to remove the spine.
3. Flip the turkey and season on both sides then place it on the preheated grill or on a pan if you want to catch the drippings.
4. Grill on high for 30 minutes, reduce the temperature to 325°F, and grill for 45 more minutes or until the internal temperature reaches 165°F
5. Remove from the grill and let rest for 20 minutes before slicing and serving. Enjoy.

Nutrition: Calories: 156 Cal Fat: 16 g Carbohydrates: 1 g Protein: 2 g Fiber: 0 g

Wood Pellet Smoked Cornish Hens

Preparation Time: 10 minutes
Cooking Time: 1 hour
Servings: 6
Ingredients:

- 6 Cornish hens
- 3 tbsp avocado oil
- 6 tbsp rub of choice

Directions:

1. Fire up the wood pellet and preheat it to 275°F.
2. Rub the hens with oil then coat generously with rub. Place the hens on the grill with the chest breast side down.
3. Smoke for 30 minutes. Flip the hens and increase the grill temperature to 400°F. Cook until the internal temperature reaches 165°F.
4. Remove from the grill and let rest for 10 minutes before serving. Enjoy.

Nutrition: Calories: 696 Cal Fat: 50 g Carbohydrates: 1 g Protein: 57 g Fiber: 0 g

Smoked and Fried Chicken Wings

Preparation Time: 10 minutes
Cooking Time: 2 hours
Servings: 6
Ingredients:

- 3 pounds chicken wings
- 1 tbsp Goya adobo all-purpose seasoning
- Sauce of your choice

Directions:

1. Fire up your wood pellet grill and set it to smoke.
2. Meanwhile, coat the chicken wings with adobo all-purpose seasoning. Place the chicken on the grill and smoke for 2 hours.
3. Remove the wings from the grill.
4. Preheat oil to 375°F in a frying pan. Drop the wings in batches and let fry for 5 minutes or until the skin is crispy.
5. Drain the oil and proceed with drizzling preferred sauce
6. Drain oil and drizzle preferred sauce
7. Enjoy.

Nutrition: Calories: 755 Cal Fat: 55 g Carbohydrates: 24 g Protein: 39 g Fiber: 1 g

TURKEY, RABBIT AND VEAL

Whole Turkey

Preparation Time: 10 Minutes

Cooking Time: 7 Hours And 30 Minutes

Servings: 10

Ingredients:

- 1 frozen whole turkey, giblets removed, thawed
- 2 tablespoons orange zest
- 2 tablespoons chopped fresh parsley
- 1 teaspoon salt
- 2 tablespoons chopped fresh rosemary
- 1 teaspoon ground black pepper
- 2 tablespoons chopped fresh sage
- 1 cup butter, unsalted, softened, divided
- 2 tablespoons chopped fresh thyme
- ½ cup water
- 14.5-ounce chicken broth

Directions:

1. Open hopper of the smoker, add dry pallets, make sure ash-can is in place, then open the ash damper, power on the smoker and close the ash damper.
2. Set the temperature of the smoker to 180 degrees F, let preheat for 30 minutes or until the green light on the dial blinks that indicate smoker has reached to set temperature.
3. Meanwhile, prepare the turkey and for this, tuck its wings under it by using kitchen twine.
4. Place ½ cup butter in a bowl, add thyme, parsley, and sage, orange zest, and rosemary, stir well until combined and then brush this mixture generously on the inside and outside of the turkey and season the external of turkey with salt and black pepper.
5. Place turkey on a roasting pan, breast side up, pour in broth and water, add the remaining butter in the pan, then place the pan on the smoker grill and shut with lid.
6. Smoke the turkey for 3 hours, then increase the temperature to 350 degrees F and continue smoking the turkey for 4 hours or until thoroughly cooked and the internal temperature of the turkey reaches to 165 degrees F, basting turkey with the dripping every 30 minutes, but not in the last hour.
7. When you are done, take off the roasting pan from the smoker and let the turkey rest for 20 minutes.
8. Carve turkey into pieces and serve.

Nutrition: Calories: 146 Fat: 8 g Protein: 18 g Carbs: 1 g

Herbed Turkey Breast

Preparation Time: 8 Hours And 10 Minutes

Cooking Time: 3 Hours
Servings: 12
Ingredients:

- 7 pounds turkey breast, bone-in, skin-on, fat trimmed
- 3/4 cup salt
- 1/3 cup brown sugar
- 4 quarts water, cold
- For Herbed Butter:
- 1 tablespoon chopped parsley
- ½ teaspoon ground black pepper
- 8 tablespoons butter, unsalted, softened
- 1 tablespoon chopped sage
- ½ tablespoon minced garlic
- 1 tablespoon chopped rosemary
- 1 teaspoon lemon zest
- 1 tablespoon chopped oregano
- 1 tablespoon lemon juice

Directions:

1. Prepare the brine and for this, pour water in a large container, add salt and sugar and stir well until salt and sugar has completely dissolved. Add turkey breast in the brine, cover with the lid and let soak in the refrigerator for a minimum of 8 hours.
2. Then remove turkey breast from the brine, rinse well and pat dry with paper towels.
3. Open hopper of the smoker, add dry pallets, make sure ash-can is in place, then open the ash damper, power on the smoker and close the ash damper.
4. Set the temperature of the smoker to 350 degrees F, let preheat for 30 minutes or until the green light on the dial blinks that indicate smoker has reached to set temperature.
5. Meanwhile, take a roasting pan, pour in 1 cup water, then place a wire rack in it and place turkey breast on it.
6. Prepare the herb butter and for this, place butter in a heatproof bowl, add remaining ingredients for the butter and stir until just mix.
7. Loosen the skin of the turkey from its breast by using your fingers, then insert 2 tablespoons of prepared herb butter on each side of the skin of the breastbone and spread it evenly, pushing out all the air pockets.
8. Place the remaining herb butter in the bowl into the microwave wave and heat for 1 minute or more at high heat setting or until melted.
9. Then brush melted herb butter on the outside of the turkey breast and place roasting pan containing turkey on the smoker grill.
10. Shut the smoker with lid and smoke for 2 hours and 30 minutes or until the turkey breast is nicely golden brown and the internal temperature of turkey reach to 165 degrees F, flipping the turkey and basting with melted herb butter after 1 hour and 30 minutes smoking. When done, transfer the turkey breast to a cutting board, let it rest for 15 minutes, then carve it into pieces and serve.

Nutrition: Calories: 97 Fat: 4 g Protein: 13 g Carbs: 1 g

Smoked Turkey Mayo with Green Apple

Preparation Time: 20 minutes

Cooking Time: 4 hours 10 minutes

Servings: 10

Ingredients:

- Whole turkey (4-lbs., 1.8-kg.)
- The Rub
- Mayonnaise – ½ cup
- Salt – ¾ teaspoon
- Brown sugar – ¼ cup
- Ground mustard – 2 tablespoons
- Black pepper – 1 teaspoon
- Onion powder – 1 ½ tablespoons
- Ground cumin – 1 ½ tablespoons
- Chili powder – 2 tablespoons
- Cayenne pepper – ½ tablespoon
- Old Bay Seasoning – ½ teaspoon
- The Filling
- Sliced green apples – 3 cups

Directions:

1. Place salt, brown sugar, brown mustard, black pepper, onion powder, ground cumin, chili powder, cayenne pepper, and old bay seasoning in a bowl then mix well. Set aside.
2. Next, fill the turkey cavity with sliced green apples then baste mayonnaise over the turkey skin.
3. Sprinkle the dry spice mixture over the turkey then wrap with aluminum foil.
4. Marinate the turkey for at least 4 hours or overnight and store in the fridge to keep it fresh.
5. On the next day, remove the turkey from the fridge and thaw at room temperature.
6. Meanwhile, plug the blackstone smoker then fill the hopper with the blackstone. Turn the switch on.
7. Set the blackstone smoker for indirect heat then adjust the temperature to 275°F (135°C).
8. Unwrap the turkey and place in the blackstone smoker.
9. Smoke the turkey for 4 hours or until the internal temperature has reached 170°F (77°C).
10. Remove the smoked turkey from the blackstone smoker and serve.

Nutrition: Calories: 340 Carbs: 40g Fat: 10g Protein: 21g

Buttery Smoked Turkey Beer

Preparation Time: 15 minutes
Cooking Time: 4 hours
Servings: 6
Ingredients:

- Whole turkey (4-lbs., 1.8-kg.)
- The Brine
- Beer – 2 cans
- Salt – 1 tablespoon
- White sugar – 2 tablespoons
- Soy sauce – ¼ cup
- Cold water – 1 quart
- The Rub
- Unsalted butter – 3 tablespoons
- Smoked paprika – 1 teaspoon
- Garlic powder – 1 ½ teaspoons
- Pepper – 1 teaspoon
- Cayenne pepper – ¼ teaspoon

Directions:

1. Pour beer into a container then add salt, white sugar, and soy sauce then stir well.
2. Put the turkey into the brine mixture cold water over the turkey. Make sure that the turkey is completely soaked.
3. Soak the turkey in the brine for at least 6 hours or overnight and store in the fridge to keep it fresh.
4. On the next day, remove the turkey from the fridge and take it out of the brine mixture.
5. Wash and rinse the turkey then pat it dry.
6. Next, plug the blackstone smoker then fill the hopper with the blackstone. Turn the switchon.
7. Set the blackstone smoker for indirect heat then adjust the temperature to 275°F (135°C).
8. Open the beer can then push it in the turkey cavity.
9. Place the seasoned turkey in the blackstone smoker and make a tripod using the beer canand the two turkey-legs.
10. Smoke the turkey for 4 hours or until the internal temperature has reached 170°F (77°C).
11. Once it is done, remove the smoked turkey from the blackstone smoker and transfer itto a serving dish.

Nutrition: Calories: 229 Carbs: 34g Fat: 8g Protein: 3g

Barbecue Chili Smoked Turkey Breast

Preparation Time: 15 minutes

Cooking Time: 4 hours 20 minutes

Servings: 8

Ingredients:

- Turkey breast (3-lb., 1.4-kg.)
- The Rub
- Salt – ¾ teaspoon
- Pepper – ½ teaspoon
- The Glaze
- Olive oil – 1 tablespoon
- Ketchup – ¾ cup
- White vinegar – 3 tablespoons
- Brown sugar – 3 tablespoons
- Smoked paprika – 1 tablespoons
- Chili powder – ¾ teaspoon
- Cayenne powder – ¼ teaspoon

Directions:

1. Score the turkey breast at several places then sprinkle salt and pepper over it.
2. Let the seasoned turkey breast rest for approximately 10 minutes.
3. In the meantime, plug the blackstone smoker then fill the hopper with the blackstone. Turn the switch on.
4. Set the blackstone smoker for indirect heat then adjust the temperature to 275°F (135°C).
5. Place the seasoned turkey breast in the blackstone smoker and smoke for 2 hours.
6. In the meantime, combine olive oil, ketchup, white vinegar, brown sugar, smoked paprika; chili powder, garlic powder, and cayenne pepper in a saucepan then stir until incorporated. Wait to simmer then remove from heat.
7. After 2 hours of smoking, baste the sauce over the turkey breast and continue smoking for another 2 hours.
8. Once the internal temperature of the smoked turkey breast has reached 170°F (77°C) remove from the blackstone smoker and wrap with aluminum foil.
9. Let the smoked turkey breast rest for approximately 15 minutes to 30 minutes then unwrap it.
10. Cut the smoked turkey breast into thick slices then serve.

Nutrition: Calories: 290 Carbs: 2g Fat: 3g Protein: 63g

Hot Sauce Smoked Turkey Tabasco

Preparation Time: 20 minutes

Cooking Time: 4 hours 15 minutes

Servings: 8

Ingredients:

- Whole turkey (4-lbs., 1.8-kg.)
- The Rub
- Brown sugar – ¼ cup
- Smoked paprika – 2 teaspoons
- Salt – 1 teaspoon
- Onion powder – 1 ½ teaspoons
- Oregano – 2 teaspoons
- Garlic powder – 2 teaspoons
- Dried thyme – ½ teaspoon
- White pepper – ½ teaspoon
- Cayenne pepper – ½ teaspoon
- The Glaze
- Ketchup – ½ cup
- Hot sauce – ½ cup
- Cider vinegar – 1 tablespoon
- Tabasco – 2 teaspoons
- Cajun spices – ½ teaspoon
- Unsalted butter – 3 tablespoons

Directions:

1. Rub the turkey with 2 tablespoons of brown sugar, smoked paprika, salt, onion powder, garlic powder, dried thyme, white pepper, and cayenne pepper. Let the turkey rest for an hour.
2. Plug the blackstone smoker then fill the hopper with the blackstone. Turn the switch on.
3. Set the blackstone smoker for indirect heat then adjust the temperature to 275°F (135°C).
4. Place the seasoned turkey in the blackstone smoker and smoke for 4 hours.
5. In the meantime, place ketchup, hot sauce, cider vinegar, Tabasco, and Cajun spices in a saucepan then bring to a simmer.
6. Remove the sauce from heat and quickly add unsalted butter to the saucepan. Stir until melted.
7. After 4 hours of smoking, baste the Tabasco sauce over the turkey then continue smoking for 15 minutes.
8. Once the internal temperature of the smoked turkey has reached 170°F (77°C), remove from the blackstone smoker and place it on a serving dish.

Nutrition: Calories: 160 Carbs: 2g Fat: 14g Protein: 7g

Cured Turkey Drumstick

Preparation Time: 20 minutes
Cooking Time: 2.5 hours to 3 hours
Servings: 3
Ingredients:

- 3 fresh or thawed frozen turkey drumsticks
- 3 tablespoons extra virgin olive oil
- Brine component
- 4 cups of filtered water
- ¼ Cup kosher salt
- ¼ cup brown sugar
- 1 teaspoon garlic powder
- Poultry seasoning 1 teaspoon
- 1/2 teaspoon red pepper flakes
- 1 teaspoon pink hardened salt

Directions:

1. Put the salt water ingredients in a 1 gallon sealable bag. Add the turkey drumstick to the salt water and refrigerate for 12 hours.
2. After 12 hours, remove the drumstick from the saline, rinse with cold water, and pat dry with a paper towel.
3. Air dry the drumstick in the refrigerator without a cover for 2 hours.
4. Remove the drumsticks from the refrigerator and rub a tablespoon of extra virgin olive oil under and over each drumstick.
5. Set the blackstone or grill for indirect cooking and preheat to 250 degrees Fahrenheit using hickory or maple blackstones.
6. Place the drumstick on the grill and smoke at 250 ° F for 2 hours.
7. After 2 hours, increase grill temperature to 325 ° F.
8. Cook the turkey drumstick at 325 ° F until the internal temperature of the thickest part of each drumstick is 180 ° F with an instant reading digital thermometer.
9. Place a smoked turkey drumstick under a loose foil tent for 15 minutes before eating.

Nutrition: Calories: 278 Carbs: 0g Fat: 13g Protein: 37g

SMOKING RECIPES

Smoked Hot Paprika Pork Tenderloin

Preparation Time: 20-35 minutes
Cooking Time: 2 ½ to 3 hours
Servings: 6
Ingredients:

- 2-pound pork tenderloin
- 3/4 cup chicken stock
- 1/2 cup tomato-basil sauce
- 2 tbsp smoked hot paprika (or to taste)
- 1 tbsp oregano
- Salt and pepper to taste

Directions:

1. In a bowl, combine the chicken stock, tomato-basil sauce, paprika, oregano, salt, and pepper together.
2. Brush over tenderloin.
3. Smoke grill for 4-5 minutes. Pre head, lid closed for 10-14 minutes
4. Place pork for 2 ½ to 3 hours.
5. Rest for 10 minutes.

Nutrition: Calories: 360.71 Cal Fat: 14.32 g Carbohydrates: 3.21 g Protein: 52.09 g Fiber: 1.45 g

Smoked Pork Tenderloin with Mexican Pineapple Sauce

Preparation Time: 10-15 minutes
Cooking Time: 3 hours and 55 minutes
Servings: 6
Ingredients:

- Pineapple Sauce
- 1 can (11 oz) unsweetened crushed pineapple
- 1 can (11 oz) roasted tomato or tomatillo
- 1/2 cup port wine
- 1/4 cup orange juice
- 1/4 cup packed brown sugar
- 1/4 cup lime juice
- 2 tbsp Worcestershire sauce
- 1 tsp garlic powder
- 1/4 tsp cayenne pepper
- PORK
- 2 pork tenderloin (1 pound each)
- 1 tsp ground cumin
- 1/2 tsp pepper
- 1/4 tsp cayenne pepper
- 2 tbsp lime juice (freshly squeezed)

Directions:

1. Combine cumin, pepper, cayenne pepper and lime juice and rub over tenderloins.
2. Smoke grill for 4-5 minutes. Preheat, lid closed for 10-15 minutes
3. Smoke tenderloin for 2 ½ to 3 hours.
4. Rest for 5 minutes
5. For Sauce:
6. Combine ingredients and boil for 25 minutes
7. Remove from heat and cool.
8. Serve pork slices with pineapple sauce and lime wedges.

Nutrition: Calories: 277.85 Cal Fat: 3.49 g Carbohydrates: 24.31 g Protein: 32.42 g Fiber: 0.67 g

Garlic Aioli and Smoked Salmon Sliders

Preparation Time: 15 minutes
Cooking Time: 1 hour and 30 minutes
Servings: 12
Ingredients:

- For Brine:
- Water as needed
- ½ a cup of salt
- 1 tablespoon of dried tarragon
- 1 and a ½ pound of salmon fillets
- For Aioli:
- 1 cup of mayonnaise
- 3 tablespoon of fresh lemon juice
- 3 minced garlic cloves
- 1 and a ½ teaspoon of ground black pepper
- ½ a teaspoon of lemon zest
- Salt as needed
- ½ a cup of apple wood chips
- 12 slide burger buns

Directions:

1. Take a large sized baking dish and add ½ a cup of salt alongside about half water
2. Add tarragon, salmon in the brine mix and keep adding more water
3. Cover up the dish and freeze for 2-12 hours. Take a small bowl and add lemon juice, mayonnaise, pepper, garlic, 1 pinch of salt and lemon zest.
4. Mix and chill for 30 minutes
5. Remove your Salmon from the brine and place it on a wire rack and let it sit for about 30 minutes.
6. Smoke them over low heat for 1 and a ½ to 2 hours. Assemble sliders by dividing the salmon among 12 individual buns.
7. Top each of the pieces with a spoonful of aioli and place another bun on top

Nutrition: Calories: 320 Cal Fat: 22 g Carbohydrates: 13 g Protein: 22 g Fiber: 0 g

Texas Styled Smoked Flounder

Preparation Time: 20 minutes
Cooking Time: 20 minutes
Servings: 6
Ingredients:

- 1 whole flounder
- 1 halved lemon
- Ground black pepper as needed
- 2 tablespoons of chopped up fresh dill
- 1 tablespoon of olive oil
- 1 cup of soaked wood chips

Directions:

1. Preheat your smoker to a temperature of 350 degrees Fahrenheit.
2. Slice half of your lemon and place them into the slices. Rub the fish with a coating of olive oil. Squeeze another half of the lemon all over the fish. Season with some black pepper.
3. Rub 1 tablespoon of dill into the slits and insert the lemon slices firmly. Place the flounder on top of a large piece of aluminum foil and fold the sides all around the fish.
4. Place the fish in your smoker and throw a couple handful of soaked wood chips into the coals. And smoke for 10 minutes
5. Once done, seal up the foil and smoke it until it is fully done. Remove fish and garnish with some extra dill

Nutrition: Calories: 226 Cal Fat: 4 g Carbohydrates: 28 g Protein: 28 g Fiber: 0 g

FISH AND SEAFOOD RECIPES

Fancy Garlic and Citrus Scallops

Preparation Time: 10 minutes
Cooking Time: 30-40 minutes
Serving: 8
Recommended Wood Type: Alder/Apple/Cherry

Ingredients

- 2-3 pounds of fresh scallops
- 1 tbsp. Of freshly squeezed lemon juice
- 1 tbsp. of freshly squeezed orange juice
- 1 tbsp. of ground black pepper
- 2 tsp. of salt
- One garlic, minced
- Zest of 1 orange

Directions:

1. Take your drip pan and add water. Cover with aluminum foil. Pre-heat your smoker to 200 degrees F
2. Use water fill water pan halfway through and place it over drip pan. Add wood chips to the side tray
3. Take a large bowl and stir in scallops with orange juice and lemon
4. Season with salt, pepper, and garlic
5. Transfer the scallops to your smoker and smoke for 30-40 minutes
6. Sprinkle zest over your scallops, and serve warm!

Nutrition: Calories: 346 Fats: 28g Carbs: 22g Fiber: 2g

Big-Shot Lobster Tails

Preparation Time: 25 minutes
Cooking Time: 60 minutes
Serving: 4
Recommended Wood Type: Alder/Oak Wood

Ingredients

- 4 tbsp. of melted butter
- One lemon juice
- 3 tsp. of fresh ground black pepper
- 3 tsp. of ground white pepper
- 2 tsp. of red pepper flakes
- One minced garlic clove
- 1 tbsp. Of lemon pepper seasoning
- Four lobster tails split at the top of the shell

Directions:

1. Take your drip pan and add water; cover with aluminum foil. Pre-heat your smoker to 225 degrees F
2. Use water fill water pan halfway through and place it over drip pan. Add wood chips to the side tray
3. Take a small bowl and stir in butter, lemon juice, red pepper flakes, black and white pepper, garlic, and lemon pepper seasoning
4. Base the lobster tail with the seasoned butter and transfer to smoker rack
5. Smoke for 30 minutes
6. Baste again, a smoker for 30 minutes more
7. Once the internal temperature reaches 140 degrees Fahrenheit
8. Remove the heat and baste for a while more
9. Serve hot and enjoy!

Nutrition: Calories: 278 Fats: 13g Carbs: 0g Fiber: 2g

Awesome Boney Shad

Preparation Time: 4 hours
Cooking Time: 3 hours
Serving: 8
Recommended Wood Type: Alder/ Apple/ Cherry

Ingredients

- 20 Shad fillets

For Brine 1

- 1 cup of kosher salt
- 2 quarts of water
- For Brine 2
- 1/2 a cup of kosher salt
- 2 quarts of water
- ½ a cup of maple syrup
- One onion, chopped
- Three garlic cloves smashed
- Juice of lemon
- 1 tbsp. of cracked black pepper
- 1 tbsp. of fennel seeds
- 2-3 crushed dried hot chilies
- Five pieces of bay leaves
- 1 tsp. Of crushed coriander seeds

Directions:

1. Mix up the ingredients listed under Brine 1 and soak your shad fillets in it for about 30 minutes
2. Drain them
3. In the meantime, prepare the second bring mix and bring it to a simmer
4. Stir well to combine everything
5. Turn off the heat
6. Set it aside to cool
7. Once the second brine is cooled down, pour it all over the shad and brine and let the rest for about 2 hours
8. Drain and rinse the fillets completely
9. Pat them dry using a kitchen towel
10. Air dry in a drafty place for about 3 hours
11. Take your drip pan and add water; cover with aluminum foil. Pre-heat your smoker to 180 degrees F
12. Use water fill water pan halfway through and place it over drip pan. Add wood chips to the side tray
13. Smoke your fillets over wood for 1-3 hours
14. Remove and let it cool
15. Serve and enjoy!

Nutrition: Calories: 1742 Fats: 132g Carbs: 47g Fiber: 10g

Lemon and Pepper Bacon Wrapped Trout

Preparation Time: 15 minutes
Cooking Time: 120 minutes
Serving: 4
Recommended Wood Type: Alder/ Apple/ Cherry

Ingredients

- Four whole trout fillets
- 1 tbsp. of freshly ground black pepper
- 2 tsp. of salt
- 4-8 bacon slices, semi-cooked
- Juice of 1 lemon
- Chopped fresh parsley leaves, garnish

Directions:

1. Take your drip pan and add water. Cover with aluminum foil. Pre-heat your smoker to 200 degrees F
2. Use water fill water pan halfway through and place it over drip pan. Add wood chips to the side tray
3. Put some seasoning to the fillets with salt and pepper, wrap each of them with 1-2 bacon slices
4. Wrap the bacon very tight and secure with a toothpick
5. Squeeze lemon juice on all sides
6. Transfer fish to your smoker and smoke for 2 to 2 and a ½ hours until the internal temperature of fish reaches 160 degree Fahrenheit
7. Sprinkle parsley and serve warm!

Nutrition: Calories: 854 Fats: 54g Carbs: 19g Fiber: 2g

Stuffed Tilapia and Shrimp

Preparation Time: 20 minutes
Cooking Time: 45 minutes
Serving: 6
Recommended Wood Type: Alder/ Apple/ Cherry

Ingredients

- 5 ounce of fresh, farmed tilapia fillets
- 2 tbsp. of extra virgin olive oil
- 1 and a ½ tsp. of smoked paprika
- 1 and a ½ tsp. of old Bay Seasoning

For Shrimp Stuffing

- 1 pound of cooked and deveined shrimp (tail off)
- 1 tbsp. of salted butter
- 1 cup of red onion, diced
- 1 cup of Italian bread crumbs
- ½ a cup of Italian bread crumbs
- ½ a cup of mayonnaise
- One beaten large eggs
- 2 tsp. of freshly chopped parsley
- 1 and a ½ tsp. of salt and pepper

Directions:

1. Take a food processor and add shrimp, chop them up
2. Take a skillet and place it over medium-high heat, add butter and allow it to melt
3. Sauté the onions for 3 minutes
4. Add chopped shrimp with cooled Sautéed onion alongside remaining ingredients listed under stuffing ingredients and transfer to a bowl
5. Cover it and allow the mix to refrigerate for 60 minutes
6. Rub both sides of the fillet with olive oil
7. Spoon 1/3 cup of the stuffing to the fillet
8. Flatten out the stuffing onto the bottom half of the fillet and fold the Tilapia in half
9. Secure with two toothpicks
10. Dust each fillet with smoked paprika and Old Bay seasoning
11. Take your drip pan and add water; cover with aluminum foil. Pre-heat your smoker to 400 degrees F
12. Use water fill water pan halfway through and place it over drip pan. Add wood chips to the side tray
13. Add your preferred wood chips and transfer the fillets to a non-stick grill tray
14. Transfer to your smoker and smoker for 30-45 minutes until the internal temperature reaches 145 degrees Fahrenheit
15. Let the fish to rest for 5 minutes and enjoy!

Nutrition: Calories: 620 Fats: 50g Carbs: 6g Fiber: 1g

Subtle Pacific Oyster

Preparation Time: 60 minutes
Cooking Time: 120 minutes
Serving: 8
Recommended Wood Type: Alder/ Apple/ Cherry

Ingredients

- 40 to 50 oysters in shells
- 1 cup of white wine
- 1 cup of water
- ¼ cup of high-quality olive oil

Directions:

1. Wash the oysters under cold water
2. Take a bowl and add white wine, water and bring to a boil
3. Add oysters in a single layer and steam for 3 minutes until the oysters are open
4. Transfer the opened oysters to a bowl and add more fresh ones to the steaming pot. Repeat until all oysters are done
5. Drain the cooking liquid through a paper towel into a bowl and keep the liquid on the side
6. Take a small bowl and sharp knife and remove the oysters from the shells, transfer the removed oysters to the bowl
7. Dip the removed oysters into the cooking liquid and keep them there for 20 minutes
8. Take your drip pan and add water; cover with aluminum foil. Pre-heat your smoker to 145 degrees F
9. Use water fill water pan halfway through and place it over drip pan. Add wood chips to the side tray
10. Transfer oysters to the middle rack (If possible, keep them on top of a grate to ensure that the oysters don't fall off)
11. Smoker for 90 to 120 minutes, making sure not to overcook them
12. Drizzle a bit of olive oil over the oysters, and enjoy!

Nutrition: Calories: 329 Fats: 15g Carbs: 34g Fiber: 3g

Peppercorn Tuna Steak

Preparation Time: 8 hours
Cooking Time: 10 minutes
Serving: 8
Recommended Wood Type: Alder/ Apple/ Cherry

Ingredients

- ¼ cup of salt
- 2 pound of yellow fin tuna
- ¼ cup of Dijon mustard
- Freshly ground black pepper
- 2 tbsp. of peppercorn

Directions:

1. Take a large-sized container and dissolve salt in warm water (enough water to cover fish)
2. Transfer tuna to the brine and cover, refrigerate for 8 hours
3. Take your drip pan and add water; cover with aluminum foil. Pre-heat your smoker to 225 degrees F
4. Use water fill water pan halfway through and place it over drip pan. Add wood chips to the side tray
5. Remove tuna from bring and pat it dry
6. Transfer to grill pan and spread Dijon mustard all over
7. Season with pepper and sprinkle peppercorn on top
8. Transfer tuna to smoker and smoker for 1 hour. Enjoy!

Nutrition: Calories: 707 Fats 57g Carbs: 10g Fiber: 2g

Smoky Texas Flounder

Preparation Time: 20 minutes
Cooking Time: 45-60 minutes
Serving: 6
Recommended Wood Type: Alder/ Apple/ Cherry

Ingredients

- One whole flounder
- 1 halved lemon
- Ground black pepper as needed
- 2 tbsp. Of chopped up fresh dill
- 1 tbsp. of olive oil

Directions:

1. Take your drip pan and add water; cover with aluminum foil. Pre-heat your smoker to 350 degrees F
2. Use water fill water pan halfway through and place it over drip pan. Add wood chips to the side tray
3. Clean up and scale your fresh flounder, making sure to leave the head
4. Take a knife and make 3-4 diagonal slits across the body that are big enough for lemon slices
5. Slice half of your lemon and place them into the slices
6. Rub the fish with a coating of olive oil
7. Squeeze another half of the lemon all over the fish
8. Season with some black pepper
9. Rub about one tablespoon of dill into the slits and insert the lemon slices firmly
10. Place the flounder on top of a large piece of aluminum foil and fold the sides all around the fish
11. Make sure that enough foil is left so that you can seal the fish in a packet
12. Place the fish in your smoker and throw a couple of handful of soaked wood chips into the coals
13. Let it smoke for about 10 minutes
14. Once done, seal up the foil and smoke it until it is entirely done (flesh should easily flake off)
15. Remove the fish from your grill and garnish with some extra dill
16. Serve!

Nutrition: Calories: 226 Fats: 4g Carbs: 28g Fiber: 5g

Crab Stuffed Tomato

Preparation Time: 10 minutes
Cooking Time: 45 minutes
Serving: 4
Recommended Wood Type: Alder/ Apple/ Cherry

Ingredients

- 1 pound of the fresh lump of crabmeat
- 2 cups of panko bread crumbs
- 1 cup of chopped scallions, with the white and green pats, moved
- Two large eggs, beaten
- ½ a cup of melted butter
- ¼ cup of freshly squeezed lemon juice
- 1 tsp. Of salt
- ½ a teaspoon of freshly ground black pepper
- Eight large tomatoes, hollowed out, making sure to leave enough flesh all around on the bottom to form a nice shell

Directions:

1. Take your drip pan and add water; cover with aluminum foil. Pre-heat your smoker to 200 degrees F
2. Use water fill water pan halfway through and place it over drip pan. Add wood chips to the side tray
3. Take a large-sized bowl and stir in crabmeat, scallions, bread crumbs, eggs, lemon juice, butter, salt, and pepper
4. Stuff the mixture into the tomatoes and transfer to the smoker
5. Smoke for 45 minutes. Enjoy!

Nutrition: Calories: 559 Fats: 5g Carbs: 57g Fiber: 1g

Hot and Cold Feisty Salmon

Preparation Time: 16 hours
Cooking Time: 8 hours
Serving: 4
Recommended Wood Type: Alder/ Apple/ Cherry

Ingredients

- 5 pound of fresh sockeye (red) salmon fillets

For trout Brine

- 4 cups of filtered water
- 1 cup of soy sauce
- ½ a cup of pickling kosher salt
- ½ a cup of brown sugar
- 2 tbsp. of garlic powder
- 2 tbsp. of onion powder
- 1 tsp. of cayenne pepper

Directions:

1. Combine all of the ingredients listed under trout brine in two different 1-gallon bags
2. Store it in your fridge
3. Cut up the Salmon fillets into 3-4 inch pieces
4. Place your salmon pieces into your 1-gallon container of trout brine and let it keep in your fridge for 8 hours
5. Rotate the Salmon from time to time
6. Remove the salmon from your brine and pat them dry using a kitchen towel
7. Air Dry the brined salmon in your fridge for 8 hours
8. Add pellets to your smoker
9. Remove your salmon pieces from your fridge and place them on a Teflon coated fiberglass
10. Take your drip pan and add water; cover with aluminum foil. Pre-heat your smoker to 180 degrees F
11. Use water fill water pan halfway through and place it over drip pan. Add wood chips to the side tray
12. Once a cold smoke of 70 degrees Fahrenheit starts to come out, smoke your salmon
13. Smoke your fillets following the specified temperatures:
14. 1 hour at 180 degrees Fahrenheit
15. 1 hour at 225 degrees Fahrenheit
16. 2 hours at 250 degrees Fahrenheit
17. 2-4 hours at 350 degrees Fahrenheit
18. Finally, keep smoking it until the internal temperature reaches 145 degrees Fahrenheit
19. Remove the Salmon from your smoker and let it rest for 10 minutes

Nutrition: Calories: 849 Fats: 45g Carbs: 51g Fiber: 0g

Cedar Plank Salmon

Preparation Time: 2 hours 10 minutes

Cooking Time: 2 hours 45 minutes

Servings: 4

Ingredients:

- 2 pounds salmon fillets
- ¼ cup brown sugar
- ¼ cup of soy sauce
- 3 tbsp. apple cider vinegar
- ¼ cup red wine
- ¼ cup sweet Thai chili sauce
- Cedar plank as needed

Directions:

1. Place sugar in a small bowl, add soy sauce, vinegar, and red wine, and stir well until combined.
2. Place salmon fillets in a large plastic bag, pour in brown sugar mixture, seal the bag, turn it upside down to coat salmon with the combination and marinate in the refrigerator for 2 hours.
3. In the meantime, soak the cider plank in the water.
4. When ready to cook, open the smoker's hopper, add dry pallets, make sure the ash-can is in place, open the ash damper, power on the smoker, and close the ash damper.
5. Set the temperature of the smoker to 20 degrees F; let preheat for 30 minutes or until the green light on the dial blinks that indicate the smoker has reached to set temperature.
6. Meanwhile, pat dries the plant, arranges marinated salmon fillets on it, and places them on the smoker grill.
7. Shut the smoker with a lid, smoke for 1 hour, then baste salmon fillets with half of the chili sauce and continue smoking for 1 hour.
8. Then, increase the smoker's temperature to 350 degrees F, baste fillets with remaining chili sauce, flip the fillets, and continue smoking the fillets until the salmon's internal temperature reaches 130 degrees F.
9. Serve straight away.

Nutrition: Calories: 370; Total Fat: 13.1 g; Saturated Fat: 1.8 g; Protein: 38.3 g; Carbs: 20.4 g; Fiber: 0.3 g; Sugar: 12.4 g

VEGETARIAN RECIPES

Georgia Sweet Onion Bake

Preparation Time: 10 Minutes
Cooking Time: 30 Minutes
Servings: 4
Ingredients:

- 4 large Vidalia or other sweet onions
- 8 tablespoons (1 stick) unsalted butter, melted
- 4 chicken bouillon cubes
- 1 cup grated Parmesan cheese

Directions:

1. Supply your smoker with blackstone and follow the manufacturer's specific start-upprocedure. Preheat, with the lid closed, to 350°F.
2. Coat a high-sided baking pan with cooking spray or butter.
3. Peel the onions and cut into quarters, separating into individual petals.
4. Spread the onions out in the prepared pan and pour the melted butter over them.
5. Crush the bouillon cubes and sprinkle over the buttery onion pieces, then top with the cheese.
6. Transfer the pan to the grill, close the lid, and smoke for 30 minutes.
7. Remove the pan from the grill, cover tightly with aluminum foil, and poke several holes all over to vent.
8. Place the pan back on the grill, close the lid, and smoke for an additional 30 to 45 minutes.
9. Uncover the onions, stir, and serve hot.

Nutrition: Calories: 50 Carbs: 4g Fiber: 2g Fat: 2.5g Protein: 2g

Roasted Okra

Preparation Time: 10 Minutes
Cooking Time: 30 Minutes
Servings: 4
Ingredients:

- 1-pound whole okra
- 2 tablespoons extra-virgin olive oil
- 2 teaspoons seasoned salt
- 2 teaspoons freshly ground black pepper

Directions:

1. Supply your smoker with blackstone and follow the manufacturer's specific start-up procedure. Preheat, with the lid closed, to 400°F. Alternatively, preheat your oven to 400°F.
2. Line a shallow rimmed baking pan with aluminum foil and coat with cooking spray.
3. Arrange the okra on the pan in a single layer. Drizzle with the olive oil, turning to coat. Season on all sides with the salt and pepper.
4. Place the baking pan on the grill grate, close the lid, and smoke for 30 minutes, or until crisp and slightly charred. Alternatively, roast in the oven for 30 minutes.
5. Serve hot.
6. Smoking Tip: Whether you make this okra in the oven or in your blackstone grill, be sureto fully preheat the oven or cook chamber for the best results.

Nutrition: Calories: 150 Carbohydrates: 15 g Protein: 79 g Sodium: 45 mg Cholesterol: 49 mg

Sweet Potato Chips

Preparation Time: 10 Minutes

Cooking Time: 12 to 15 Minutes

Servings: 4

Ingredients:

- 2 sweet potatoes
- 1-quart warm water
- 1 tablespoon cornstarch, plus 2 teaspoons
- ¼ cup extra-virgin olive oil
- 1 tablespoon salt
- 1 tablespoon packed brown sugar
- 1 teaspoon ground cinnamon
- 1 teaspoon freshly ground black pepper
- ½ teaspoon cayenne pepper

Directions:

1. Using a mandolin, thinly slice the sweet potatoes.
2. Pour the warm water into a large bowl and add 1 tablespoon of cornstarch and the potato slices. Let soak for 15 to 20 minutes.
3. Supply your smoker with blackstone and follow the manufacturer's specific start-up procedure. Preheat, with the lid closed, to 375°F.
4. Drain the potato slices, then arrange in a single layer on a perforated pizza pan or a baking sheet lined with aluminum foil. Brush the potato slices on both sides with the olive oil.
5. In a small bowl, whisk together the salt, brown sugar, cinnamon, black pepper, cayenne pepper, and the remaining 2 teaspoons of cornstarch. Sprinkle this seasoning blend on both sides of the potatoes.
6. Place the pan or baking sheet on the grill grate, close the lid, and smoke for 35 to 45 minutes, flipping after 20 minutes, until the chips curl up and become crispy.
7. Store in an airtight container.
8. Ingredient Tip: Avoid storing your sweet potatoes in the refrigerator's produce bin, which tends to give them a hard center and an unpleasant flavor. What, you don't have a root cellar? Just keep them in a cool, dry area of your kitchen.

Nutrition: Calories: 150 Carbohydrates: 15 g Protein: 79 g Sodium: 45 mg Cholesterol: 49 mg

Southern Slaw

Preparation Time: 10 Minutes

Cooking Time: 12 to 14 Minutes

Servings: 4

Ingredients:

- 1 head cabbage, shredded
- ¼ cup white vinegar
- ¼ cup sugar
- 1 teaspoon paprika
- ½ teaspoon salt
- ½ teaspoon freshly ground black pepper
- 1 cup heavy (whipping) cream

Directions:

1. Place the shredded cabbage in a large bowl.
2. In a small bowl, combine the vinegar, sugar, paprika, salt, and pepper.
3. Pour the vinegar mixture over the cabbage and mix well.
4. Fold in the heavy cream and refrigerate for at least 1 hour before serving.

Nutrition: Calories: 130 Carbohydrates: 5 g Protein: 79 g Sodium: 45 mg Cholesterol: 19 mg

Blackstone Grilled Zucchini Squash Spears

Preparation Time: 5 minutes,
Cooking Time: 10 minutes.
Servings: 5
Ingredients:

- 4 zucchinis, cleaned and ends cut
- 2 tbsp. olive oil
- 1 tbsp. sherry vinegar
- 2 thyme leaves pulled
- Salt and pepper to taste

Directions:

1. Cut the zucchini into halves then cut each half thirds.
2. Add the rest of the ingredients in a zip lock bag with the zucchini pieces. Toss to mix well.
3. Preheat the blackstone temperature to 350°F with the lid closed for 15 minutes.
4. Remove the zucchini from the bag and place them on the grill grate with the cut side down.
5. Cook for 4 minutes until the zucchini are tender
6. Remove from grill and serve with thyme leaves. Enjoy.

Nutrition: Calories: 74 Fat: 5.4g Carbs: 6.1g Protein: 2.6g Sugar: 3.9g Fiber: 2.3g Sodium: 302mg Potassium: 599mg:

Whole Roasted Cauliflower with Garlic Parmesan Butter

Preparation Time: 15 minutes
Cooking Time: 45 minutes
Servings: 5
Ingredients:

- 1/4 cup olive oil
- Salt and pepper to taste
- 1 cauliflower, fresh
- 1/2 cup butter, melted
- 1/4 cup parmesan cheese, grated
- 2 garlic cloves, minced
- 1/2 tbsp. parsley, chopped

Directions:

1. Preheat the blackstone grill with the lid closed for 15 minutes.
2. Meanwhile, brush the cauliflower with oil then season with salt and pepper.
3. Place the cauliflower in a cast Iron: and place it on a grill grate.
4. Cook for 45 minutes or until the cauliflower is golden brown and tender
5. Meanwhile, mix butter, cheese, garlic, and parsley in a mixing bowl.
6. In the last 20 minutes of cooking, add the butter mixture.
7. Remove the cauliflower and top with more cheese and parsley if you desire. Enjoy.

Nutrition: Calories: 156 Fat: 11.1g Carbs: 8.8g Protein: 8.2g Fiber: 3.7g Sodium: 316mg Potassium: 468.2mg

Blackstone Cold Smoked Cheese

Preparation Time: 5 minutes
Cooking Time: 2 minutes
Servings: 10
Ingredients:

- Ice
- 1 aluminum pan, full-size and disposable
- 1 aluminum pan, half-size, and disposable
- Toothpicks
- A block of cheese

Directions:

1. Preheat the blackstone to 165°F with the lid closed for 15 minutes.
2. Place the small pan in the large pan. Fill the surrounding of the small pan with ice.
3. Place the cheese in the small pan on top of toothpicks then place the pan on the grill and close the lid.
4. Smoke cheese for 1 hour, flip the cheese, and smoke for 1 more hour with the lid closed.
5. Remove the cheese from the grill and wrap it in parchment paper. Store in the fridge for 2 3 days for the smoke flavor to mellow.
6. Remove from the fridge and serve. Enjoy.

Nutrition: Calories: 1910 Total Fat: 7g Saturated Fat: 6g Total Carbs: 2g Net Carbs: 2g Protein: 6g Sugar: 1g Fiber: 0g Sodium: 340mg Potassium: 0mg

Blackstone Grilled Asparagus and Honey Glazed Carrots

Preparation Time: 15 minutes
Cooking Time: 35 minutes
Servings: 5
Ingredients:

- 1 bunch asparagus, trimmed ends
- 1 lb. carrots, peeled
- 2 tbsp. olive oil
- Sea salt to taste
- 2 tbsp. honey
- Lemon zest

Directions:

1. Sprinkle the asparagus with oil and sea salt. Drizzle the carrots with honey and salt.
2. Preheat the blackstone to 165°F with the lid closed for 15 minutes.
3. Place the carrots in the blackstone and cook for 15 minutes. Add asparagus and cook for20 more minutes or until cooked through.
4. Top the carrots and asparagus with lemon zest. Enjoy.

Nutrition: Calories: 1680 Total Fat: 30g Saturated Fat: 2g Total Carbs: 10g Net Carbs: 10g Protein: 4g Sodium: 514mg

Blackstone Smoked Asparagus

Preparation Time: 5 minutes
Cooking Time: 1 hour
Servings: 4
Ingredients:

- 1 bunch fresh asparagus ends cut
- 2 tbsp. olive oil
- Salt and pepper to taste

Directions:

1. Fire up your blackstone smokerto 230°F
2. Place the asparagus in a mixing bowl and drizzle with olive oil. Season with salt and pepper.
3. Place the asparagus in a tinfoil sheet and fold the sides such that you create a basket.
4. Smoke the asparagus for 1 hour or until soft turning after half an hour.
5. Remove from the grill and serve. Enjoy.

Nutrition: Calories: 43 Total Fat: 2g Total Carbs: 4g Net Carbs: 2g Protein: 3g Sugar: 2g Fiber: 2g Sodium: 148mg

Blackstone Smoked Acorn Squash

Preparation Time: 10 minutes
Cooking Time: 2 hours
Servings: 6
Ingredients:

- 3 tbsp. olive oil
- 3 acorn squash, halved and seeded
- 1/4 cup unsalted butter
- 1/4 cup brown Sugar:
- 1 tbsp. cinnamon, ground
- 1 tbsp. chili powder
- 1 tbsp. nutmeg, ground

Directions:

1. Brush olive oil on the acorn squash cut sides then covers the halves with foil. Poke holes on the foil to allow steam and smoke through.
2. Fire up the blackstone to 225°F and smoke the squash for 1 ½-2 hours.
3. Remove the squash from the smoker and allow it to sit.
4. Meanwhile, melt butter, Sugar: and spices in a saucepan. Stir well to combine.
5. Remove the foil from the squash and spoon the butter mixture in each squash half. Enjoy.

Nutrition: Calories: 149 Total Fat: 10g Saturated Fat: 5g Total Carbs: 14g Net Carbs: 12g Protein: 2g Sugar: 0g Fiber: 2g Sodium: 19mg Potassium: 0mg

VEGAN RECIPES

Smoked Tomatillo Salsa

Preparation Time: 15 minutes

Cooking Time: 1 Hour and 30 Minutes
Servings: 6
Ingredients:

THE VEGETABLE

- Tomatillos – 6

THE SEASONING

- Salt – 1 teaspoon
- Ground black pepper – ¾ teaspoon

THE SALSA

- Chopped cilantro – ¼ cup
- Salt – 1 teaspoon
- Ground black pepper – 1 teaspoon
- Apple cider vinegar – 1/3 cup
- Water – 3 tablespoons

Directions:

1. In the meantime, prepare tomatillos.
2. For this, remove casing of tomatillos, then cut into quarters and then place in a sheet pan.
3. Sprinkle with salt and black pepper and toss to coat.
4. When ready to smoke, place a prepared pouch of woodchips over charcoal and when start to smoke, brush the smoking grate with oil generously, place sheet pan containing tomatillos on the grate above the drip pan.
5. Set lid on smoker and monitor temperature through temperature gauge or temperature probes and maintain it.
6. Close down the lower air vent if the temperature is above 250 degrees or open up the lower air vent if the temperature drops below 255 degrees F and add few more hot coals.
7. Check every hour if more water needs to add in the drip pan and add more hot coals using tongs along with another pouch of wood chips to keep the smoke going.
8. Let smoke for 1 hour and 30 minutes or until tender and roasted.
9. When done, remove sheet pan from the smoker and transfer tomatillos into a blender.
10. Add ingredients for salsa and pulse for 2 to 3 minutes at high speed or until smooth.
11. Serve salsa with meats.

Blackstone Smoked Jalapeño Pop

Preparation Time: 15 minutes

Cooking Time: 1 Hour and 45 Minutes
Servings: 6
Ingredients:

THE VEGETABLE

- Medium jalapeno peppers, halved lengthwise – 10

OTHER Ingredients:

- Slices of bacon, thick cut – 4
- Grated cheddar cheese – 1 cup
- Cream cheese, softened – 4 ounces

Directions:

1. Place a prepared pouch of woodchips over charcoal and when start to smoke, place slices of bacon on the grate above the drip pan.
2. Close down the lower air vent if the temperature is above 250 degrees or open up the lower air vent if the temperature drops below 255 degrees F and add few more hot coals.
3. Let smoke for 1 hour or until crispy.
4. In the meantime, cut each jalapeno pepper in half and remove its seeds and ribs.
5. Arrange these pepper halves on a sheet tray in a single layer and set aside until required.
6. When bacon is done, chop it finely and transfer to a bowl.
7. Add cheeses and stir until well mixed.
8. Stuff this mixture into jalapeno peppers, about 1 tablespoon per pepper and then place a sheet pan on the smoker.
9. Let smoke for 30 to 45 minutes or until cheese melt completely and peppers are slightly roasted.
10. Serve straightaway.

RED MEAT RECIPES

Ground Lamb Kebabs

Preparation Time: 10 minutes
Cooking Time: 1 hour
Servings: 2-4
Ingredients:

The Meat

- Ground Lamb – 1-1/2 lb.

The Mixture

- Minced onions – 1/3 cup.
- Minced garlic – ½ cloves.
- Cilantro – 3 tbsp.
- Minced fresh mint – 1 tbsp.
- Ground cumin 1 tsp.
- Paprika – 1 tsp.
- Salt – 1 tsp.
- Ground coriander – ½ tsp.
- Cinnamon – ¼ tsp.
- Pita bread - to serve.

The Fire

- Wood pellet smoker, cherry wood pellets.

Directions:

1. Take a large mixing bowl. Put in all of the ingredients except for the pita bread. Now start making meatballs out of the mixture. The meatballs should be about 2 inches in diameter.
2. Take a bamboo skewer for each of the meatballs. Now, wet your hands to easily mold the skewered meal. Mold them each into a cigar shape.
3. Place it in the refrigerator for at least 30 minutes at least or preferably overnight. Set your wood pellet smoker on the smoke option and with the lid open the fire establishes. It takes about 4-5 minutes.
4. Then after that set the temperature to 350F and preheat it for about 10-15 minutes. During preheating keep the lid closed. Place the kebabs on the grill.
5. After 30 minutes turn them over.
6. Also, if the internal temperature reads 160F then it is time to turn them over. Warm the bread before serving it with kebobs.

Nutrition: Energy (calories): 173 kcal Protein: 17.62 g Fat: 10.76 g Carbohydrates: 1.72 g

Lamb Lollipops with Mango Chutney

Preparation Time: 10 minutes
Cooking Time: 1 hour
Servings: 4-6
Ingredients:

The Meat

- 6 Lamb chops (frenched) – (3/4 inch thick).

The Mixture

- Olive oil – 2 tbsp.
- Kosher salt – ½ tsp.

For Mango chutney

- 1 chopped mango.
- 3 Garlic cloves (chopped).
- ½ chopped habanero pepper.
- Salt – 1 tsp.
- Fresh lime juice – 1 tbsp.
- Chopped fresh cilantro – 3 sprigs.
- Pepper – ½ tsp.

The Fire

- Wood pellet smoker, apple wood pellets.

Directions:

1. Put all the ingredients and mix the chutney and put them in a food processor. Pulse them till you get your desired consistency. Set this aside.
2. With the lid open, establish fire in your wood pellet smoker for about 4-5 minutes. Then preheat it at a high temperature.
3. Let the lid closed for about 15 minutes of preheating. Put the lamb chops on a baking sheet and drizzle olive oil on it. Then season with salt and pepper. Allow them to sit for 10 minutes at room temperature. On the grill grate place your lamb chops. Now close the lid and grill for 5 minutes.
4. Then flip the chops over and allow them to smoke for another 3 minutes. If you want precise internal temperature, it should be 130 F to indicate that it is cooked through.
5. Remove the meat from the grill after that. Allow it to rest at least 10 minutes before serving them with the delicious chutney and sprinkled chopped mint.

Nutrition: Energy (calories): 690 kcal Protein: 90.91 g Fat: 35.74 g Carbohydrates: 1.46 g

BAKING RECIPES

Delicious Grilled Chicken Sandwich

Preparation Time: 15 minutes
Cooking Time: 50 minutes
Servings: 4
Ingredients

- 1/4 cup of mayonnaise
- 1 tablespoon of Dijon mustard
- 1 tablespoon of honey
- 4 boneless and skinless chicken breasts
- 1/2 teaspoon of steak seasoning
- 4 slices of American Swiss cheese
- 4 hamburger buns
- 2 bacon strips
- Lettuce leaves and tomato slices

Directions:

1. Using a small mixing bowl, add in the mayonnaise, mustard, and honey then mix properly to combine.
2. Use a meat mallet to pound the chicken into even thickness then slice into four parts. Season the chicken with the steak seasoning then set aside.
3. Preheat a Blackstone Smoker and Grill to 350 degrees F for about ten to fifteen minutes with its lid closed.
4. Place the seasoned chicken on the grill and grill for about twenty-five to thirty minutes until it reads an internal temperature of 165 degrees F. Grill the bacon until crispy then crumble.
5. Add the cheese on the chicken and cook for about one minute until it melts completely. At the same time, grill the buns for about one to two minutes until it is toasted as desired.
6. Place the chicken on the buns, top with the grilled bacon, mayonnaise mixture, lettuce, and tomato then serve.

Nutrition: Calories 410 cal Fat 17g Carbohydrate 29g Fiber 3g Protein 34g

Quick Yeast Dinner Rolls

Preparation Time: 5 minutes
Cooking Time: 30 minutes
Servings 8
Ingredients:

- 2 tablespoons yeast, quick rise
- 1 cup water, lukewarm
- 3 cups flour
- ¼ cup sugar
- 1 teaspoon salt
- ¼ cup unsalted butter, softened
- 1 egg
- Cooking spray, as needed
- 1 egg, for egg wash

Directions:

1. Combine the yeast and warm water in a small bowl to activate the yeast. Let sit for about 5 to 10 minutes, or until foamy.
2. Combine the flour, sugar, and salt in the bowl of a stand mixer fitted with the dough hook. Pour the water and yeast into the dry ingredients with the machine running on low speed.
3. Add the butter and egg and mix for 10 minutes, gradually increasing the speed from low to high.
4. Form the dough into a ball and place in a buttered bowl. Cover with a cloth and let the dough rise for approximately 40 minutes.
5. Transfer the risen dough to a lightly floured work surface and divide into 8 pieces, forming a ball with each.
6. Lightly spritz a cast iron pan with cooking spray and arrange the balls in the pan. Cover with a cloth and let rise for 20 minutes.
7. When ready to cook, set Blackstone temperature to 375 F (191 C) and preheat, lid closedfor 15 minutes.
8. Brush the rolls with the egg wash. Place the pan on the grill and bake for 30 minutes, or until lightly browned.
9. Remove from the grill. Serve hot.

Baked Cornbread with Honey Butter

Preparation Time: 10 minutes
Cooking Time: 35 to 45 minutes
Servings 6
Ingredients:

- 4 ears whole corn
- 1 cup all-purpose flour
- 1 cup cornmeal
- 2/3 cup white sugar
- 1½ teaspoons baking powder
- ½ teaspoon baking soda
- ½ teaspoon salt
- 1 cup buttermilk
- ½ cup butter, softened
- 2 eggs
- ½ cup butter, softened
- ¼ cup honey

Directions:

1. When ready to cook, set Blackstone temperature to High and preheat, lid closed for 15minutes.
2. Peel back the outer layer of the corn husk, keeping it attached to the cob. Remove the silk from the corn and place the husk back into place. Soak the corn in cold water for 10 minutes.
3. Place the corn directly on the grill grate and cook for 15 to 20 minutes, or until the kernels are tender, stirring occasionally. Remove from the grill and set aside.
4. In a large bowl, stir together the flour, cornmeal, sugar, baking powder, baking soda and salt.
5. In a separate bowl, whisk together the buttermilk, butter, and eggs. Pour the wet mixture into the cornmeal mixture and fold together until there are no dry spots. Pour the batter into a greased baking dish.
6. Cut the kernels from the corn and sprinkle over the top of the batter, pressing the kernels down with a spoon to submerge.
7. Turn Blackstone temperature down to 350 F (177 C). Place the baking dish on the grill. Bake for about 20 to 25 minutes, or until the top is golden brown and a toothpick inserted into the middle of the cornbread comes out clean.
8. Remove the cornbread from the grill and let cool for 10 minutes before serving.
9. To make the honey butter, mix the butter and honey until combined. Serve the cornbread with the honey butter.

CHEESE AND BREAD

<u>Baked Cherry Cheesecake Galette</u>

Preparation Time: 10 minutes
Cooking Time: 20 minutes
Servings: 6-8
Ingredients:

- For the cherry filling:
- 1-pound cherries (thawed, drained)
- ¼ cup of sugar
- 1 tsp. cornstarch
- 1 tsp. coriander
- A pinch of salt
- 1 tbsp. orange zest
- ½ tablespoon lemon zest
- For the cream cheese filling:
- 8 ounces of cream cheese (softened)
- 1 tsp. vanilla
- ¼ cup of sugar
- One egg
- For the galette:
- One refrigerated pie crust
- 1 egg, 1 tbsp. water, cream, or milk
- Granulated sugar
- Vanilla ice cream to serve

Directions:

1. Grab a medium bowl; mix your cherries, orange zest, lemon zest, and coriander, half of the sugar, cornstarch, and a pinch of salt.
2. Grab another bowl, and in it, mix your egg, vanilla, and cream cheese. Whip it up.
3. Get your pie dough onto a sheet tray, and then stretch it out with a rolling pin. Get it to about 1 inch in diameter.
4. Spread out your cream cheese filling in the middle of the pie dough. Be careful to leave a border of an inch around the edge. Then pile your cherry mix on the cream cheese.
5. Now, you're going to fold in the pie dough's edges into little parts over the filling.
6. Next, brush the edges of the pie dough with egg wash, and then sprinkle on some granulated sugar.

On the Grill:

1. Set up your wood pellet smoker grill for indirect cooking.

2. Preheat your wood pellet smoker grill at a temperature of 350 degrees Fahrenheit, keeping it closed for 15 minutes.
3. Set your sheet to try right on the grill grate, and then bake that yummy goodness for 15 to 20 minutes. You want the crust to become nice and golden brown and for the cheesecake filling to be completely set.
4. Dish the galette while warm with some ice cream. And then enjoy.

Nutrition: Calories: 400 Cal Fat: 51 g Carbohydrates: 18 g Protein: 5 g Fiber: 3 g

Smoked Mac and Cheese

Preparation Time: 2 minutes
Cooking Time: 1 hour
Servings: 2
Ingredients

- 1/2 cup butter, salted
- 1/3 cup flour
- 1/2 tbsp salt
- 6 cups whole milk
- Dash of Worcestershire
- 1/2 tbsp dry mustard
- 1 lb small cooked shells, al dente in well-salted water
- 2 cups white cheddar, smoked
- 2 cups cheddar jack cheese
- 1 cup crushed ritz

Directions:

1. Set your grill on "smoke" and run for about 5-10 minutes with the lid open until fire establishes. Now turn your grill to 325 oF then close the lid.
2. Melt butter in a saucepan, medium, over low--medium heat then whisk in flour.
3. Cook while whisking for about 5-6 minutes over low heat until light tan color.
4. Whisk in salt, milk, Worcestershire, and mustard over low-medium heat stirring frequently until a thickened sauce.
5. Stir noodles, small shells, white sauce, and 1 cup cheddar cheese in a large baking dish, 10x3" high-sided, coated with butter.
6. Top with 1 cup cheddar cheese and ritz.
7. Place on the grill and bake for about 25-30 minutes until a bubbly mixture and cheese melts.
8. Serve immediately. Enjoy!

Nutrition: Calories 628, Total fat 42g, Saturated fat 24g, Total carbs 38g, Net carbs 37g, Protein 25g, Sugars 11g, Fiber 1g, Sodium 807mg, Potassium 699mg

APPETIZERS AND SIDES

Camembert with Pepper Jelly

Preparation time: 10 minutes
Cooking time: 10 minutes
Servings 4
Ingredients;

- 1 Camembert or small Brie cheese (8 ounces / 227 g)
- 3 tablespoons pepper jelly, tomato jam, or apricot jam
- 1 large jalapeño pepper, stemmed and thinly sliced crosswise
- Grilled or toasted baguette slices or favorite crackers, for serving

Directions:

1. Set up your grill for smoke-roasting and preheat to medium-high 400°F (204°C).
2. If you're charring the plank (this step is optional, but it gives you a lot more flavor), place it directly over the fire and grill until singed on both sides, 1 to 2 minutes per side. Set aside and let cool.
3. Place the cheese in the center of the plank. Spread the top with pepper jelly using the back of a spoon. Shingle the jalapeño slices on top so they overlap in a decorative pattern.
4. Place the plank on the grill away from the heat and toss the wood chips or chunks on the coals. Smoke-roast the cheese until the sides are soft and beginning to bulge, 6 to 10 minutes.
5. Serve the cheese on the plank, hot off the grill, with a basket of grilled baguette slices or your favorite crackers.

Nutrition: Calories: 57 Total Fat: 3 g Saturated Fat: 1 g Total Carbs: 6 g Net Carbs: 4 g Protein: 4 g Sugars: 2 g Fiber: 2 g Sodium: 484 mg

Homemade Cheese

Preparation time: 5 minutes
Cooking time: 2 to 4 minutes
Servings 2 to 3

Ingredients:

- Vegetable oil, for oiling the grate
- 1 ball (8 to 12 ounces / 227 to 340 g) fresh Mozzarella, patted dry
- Extra virgin olive oil (optional)
- Coarse salt (sea or kosher) or fleur de sel, to taste (optional)

Directions:

1. Place a small mound of charcoal in the smoker firebox or to one side of a kettle grill and light it. Brush and oil the grate. When the coals glow red, place the cheese in the smoke chamber (or on the side of the kettle grill opposite the embers), as far away as possible from the fire. Toss the hay on the coals and close the smoker or cover the grill. Smoke the cheese until it's colored with smoke (but not long enough to melt it), 2 to 4 minutes.
2. Slide a spatula under the cheese and transfer it to a plate to cool. Do not grab it when hot, or the deposit of smoke will come off on your fingers. Serve once it has cooled to room temperature, or refrigerate until serving. (For maximum flavor, let the cheese warm to room temperature before serving.) Drizzle with olive oil and/or salt, if desired, and serve.

Nutrition: Calories: 57 Total Fat: 3 g Saturated Fat: 1 g Total Carbs: 6 g Net Carbs: 4 g Protein: 4 g Sugars: 2 g Fiber: 2 g Sodium: 484 mg

Syrupy Bacon Pig Pops

Preparation time: 15 minutes
Cooking time: 25 to 30 minutes
Servings 24

Ingredients:

- Nonstick cooking spray, oil, or butter, for greasing
- 2 pounds (907 g) thick-cut bacon (24 slices)
- 24 metal skewers
- 1 cup packed light brown sugar
- 2 to 3 teaspoons cayenne pepper
- ½ cup maple syrup, divided

Directions:

1. Supply your smoker with wood pellets and follow the manufacturer's specific start-up procedure. Preheat, with the lid closed, to 350°F (177°C).
2. Coat a disposable aluminum foil baking sheet with cooking spray, oil, or butter.
3. Thread each bacon slice onto a metal skewer and place on the prepared baking sheet.
4. In a medium bowl, stir together the brown sugar and cayenne.
5. Baste the top sides of the bacon with ¼ cup of maple syrup.
6. Sprinkle half of the brown sugar mixture over the bacon.
7. Place the baking sheet on the grill, close the lid, and smoke for 15 to 30 minutes.
8. Using tongs, flip the bacon skewers. Baste with the remaining ¼ cup of maple syrup and top with the remaining brown sugar mixture.
9. Continue smoking with the lid closed for 10 to 15 minutes, or until crispy. You can eyeball the bacon and smoke to your desired doneness, but the actual ideal internal temperature for bacon is 155°F (68°C) (if you want to try to get a thermometer into it—ha!).
   Using tongs, carefully remove the bacon skewers from the grill. Let cool completely before handling.

Nutrition: Calories: 57 Total Fat: 3 g Saturated Fat: 1 g Total Carbs: 6 g Net Carbs: 4 g Protein: 4 g Sugars: 2 g Fiber: 2 g Sodium: 484 mg

MORE SIDES

Mesmerizing Banana Foster

Preparation Time: 10-15 minutes
Cooking Time: 15-20 minutes
Servings: 4

Ingredients

- 10 bananas, overripe, peeled and halved lengthwise
- Rum and raisin sauce for serving

Directions:

1. Take your drip pan and add water, cover with aluminum foil. Pre-heat your smoker to 250 degrees F
2. Use water fill water pan halfway through and place it over drip pan. Add wood chips to the side tray
3. Take a large-sized disposable aluminum foil, arrange bananas in a single layer
4. Transfer to smoker and smoke for 15-20 minutes
5. Serve with rum and raisin sauce, enjoy!

Nutrition: Calories: 355 Fat: 12g Carbohydrates: 41g Protein: 1g

Stuffed Up Chorizo Pepper

Preparation Time: 10-15 minutes
Cooking Time: 2 hours
Servings: 4

Ingredients

- 3 cups cheese, shredded
- 2 pounds chorizo, ground
- 4 poblano pepper, halved and seeded
- 8 bacon slices, uncooked

Directions:

1. Take your drip pan and add water, cover with aluminum foil. Pre-heat your smoker to 225 degrees F
2. Use water fill water pan halfway through and place it over drip pan. Add wood chips to the side tray
3. Divide the mix into 8 portions and press one portion into each pepper half
4. Sprinkle rest of the cheddar on top
5. Wrap each pepper half with 1 bacon slice, making sure to tuck in the edges to secure it
6. Transfer peppers to your smoker and smoke for 2 hours until the internal temperature of the sausage reach 165-degree Fahrenheit
7. Enjoy!

Nutrition: Calories: 834 Fats: 51g Carbs: 55g Fiber: 2g

Cool Brie Cheese

Preparation Time: 10-15 minutes
Cooking Time: 60 minutes
Servings: 4
Ingredients

- 8-ounce blocks of brie cheese

Directions:

1. Take your drip pan and add water, cover with aluminum foil. Pre-heat your smoker to 90 degrees Flow settings
2. Use water fill water pan halfway through and place it over drip pan. Add wood chips to the side tray
3. Add cheese blocks to your smoker and let them smoke for 4 hours
4. Remove from heat and let them cool at room temperature
5. Transfer to a container, serve, and enjoy!

Nutrition: Calories: 100 Fat: 9g Carbohydrates: 0g Protein: 4g

SNACKS

Cajun Artichokes

Preparation Time: 30 mins.
Cooking Time: 2 hrs.
Servings: 4

Ingredients:

- 1 2-16 canned, whole artichoke hearts
- Cajun seasoning – 2 tablespoons
- Hickory wood pellets

Directions:

1. Preheat the smoker, for cold smoking
2. Slice the artichoke hearts in half.
3. Toss the artichoke halves in the Cajun seasoning.
4. Spread the hearts in a single layer on the smoker rack and cold smoke for 2 hours.
5. Serve and enjoy.

Nutrition: Calories: 25 Protein: 3g Carbs: 9g Fat: 0g

Grilled French Dip

Preparation Time: 15 Minutes
Cooking Time: 35 Minutes
Servings: 8 to 12
Ingredients:

- 3 lbs. onions, thinly sliced (yellow)
- 2 tbsp. oil
- 2 tbsp. of Butter
- Salt to taste
- Black pepper to taste
- 1 tsp. Thyme, chopped
- 2 tsp. of Lemon juice
- 1 cup Mayo
- 1 cup of Sour cream

Directions:

1. Preheat the grill to high with closed lid.
2. In a pan combine the oil and butter. Place on the grill to melt. Add 2 tsp. salt and add the onions.
3. Stir well and close the lid of the grill. Cook 30 minutes stirring often.
4. Add the thyme. Cook for an additional 3 minutes. Set aside and add black pepper.
5. Once cooled add lemon juice, mayo, and sour cream. Stir to combine. Taste and add more black pepper and salt if needed.
6. Serve with veggies or chips. Enjoy!

Nutrition: Calories: 60 Protein: 4g Carbs: 5g Fat: 6g

DESSERT RECIPE

Rum-Soaked Grilled Pineapple Sundaes

Preparation time: 15 minutes
Cooking time: 8 minutes
Servings: 6
Ingredients:

- ½ cup dark rum
- ½ cup packed brown sugar
- One teaspoon ground cinnamon, plus more for garnish
- One pineapple, cored and sliced
- Vanilla ice cream, for serving

Directions:

1. In a large shallow bowl or storage container, combine the rum, sugar, and cinnamon. Add the pineapple slices and arrange them in a single layer. Coat with the mixture, then let soak for at least 5 minutes per side.
2. Insert the Grill Grate and cover the hood. Select GRILL, then set the temperature to MAX, and set the time to 8 minutes. Select START/STOP to begin preheating.
3. While the unit is preheating, strain the extra rum sauce from the pineapple.
4. When the unit beeps to it is a sign that it has preheated, place the fruit on the Grill Grate in a single layer (you may need to do this in multiple batches). Gently press the fruit down to maximize grill marks. Close the hood and grill for about 6 to 8 minutes without flipping. If working in batches, remove the pineapple, and repeat this step for the remaining pineapple slices.
5. When cooking is complete, remove, and top each pineapple ring with a scoop of ice cream. Sprinkle with cinnamon and serve immediately.

Nutrition: Calories: 240 Saturated fat: 2g Carbohydrates: 43g Protein: 2g

Charred Peaches with Bourbon Butter Sauce

Preparation time: 10 minutes
Cooking time: 12 minutes
Servings: 4
Ingredients:

- Four tablespoons salted butter
- ¼ cup bourbon
- ½ cup brown sugar
- Four ripe peaches halved and pitted
- ¼ cup candied pecans

Directions

1. Insert the Grill Grate and cover the hood. Select GRILL, then set the temperature to MAX, and set the time to 12 minutes. Select START/STOP to begin preheating.
2. While the unit is preheating, in a saucepan over medium heat, melt the butter for about 5 minutes. Once the butter is browned, remove the pan from the heat and carefully add the bourbon.
3. Return the saucepan into medium-high heat and add the brown sugar. Bring to a boil and let the sugar dissolve for 5 minutes, stirring occasionally.
4. Pour the bourbon butter sauce into a medium shallow bowl and arrange the peaches cut side down to coat in the sauce.
5. When the unit beeps a sign that it has preheated, place the fruit on the Grill Grate in a single layer (you may need to do this in multiple batches). Gently press the fruit down to maximize grill marks. Close the hood and grill for 10 to 12 minutes without flipping. If working in batches, repeat this step for all the peaches.
6. When cooking is complete, remove the peaches and top each with the pecans. Drizzle with the remaining bourbon butter sauce and serve immediately.

Nutrition: Calories: 309 Saturated fat: 8g Carbohydrates: 34g Protein: 2g

Chocolate-Hazelnut and Strawberry Grilled Dessert Pizza

Preparation time: 10 minutes
Total cooking time: 6 minutes
Servings: 4

Ingredients:

- 2 tbsp. all-purpose flour, plus more as needed
- ½ store-bought pizza dough (about 8 ounces)
- 1 tbsp. canola oil
- 1 cup sliced fresh strawberries
- 1 tbsp. sugar
- ½ cup chocolate-hazelnut spread

Directions:

1. Insert the Grill Grate and cover the hood. Select GRILL, then set the temperature to MAX, and set the time to 6 minutes. Select START/STOP to begin preheating.
2. While the unit is preheating, dust a clean work surface with the flour, place the dough on the floured surface and roll it out to a 9-inch round of even thickness. Sprinkle the roller and work surface with additional flour, as needed, to ensure the dough does not stick.
3. Brush the surface of the rolled-out dough evenly with half the oil. Flip the dough over, and brush with the remaining oil. Poke the dough with a fork 5 or 6 times across its surface to prevent air pockets from forming during cooking.
4. When the unit beeps to signify it has preheated, place the dough on the Grill Grate. Close the hood and cook for 3 minutes.
5. After 3 minutes, flip the dough. Close the hood and continue cooking for the remaining 3 minutes.
6. Meanwhile, in a medium mixing bowl, combine the strawberries and sugar.
7. Move the pizza to a cutting board and let cool. Top with the chocolate-hazelnut spread and strawberries. Cut into pieces and serve.

Nutrition: Calories: 377 Saturated fat: 4g Sodium: 258mg Carbohydrates: 53g Protein: 7g

Bacon and Chocolate Cookies

Preparation time: 20 minutes
Total cooking time: 10-12minutes
Servings: 2 ounces cookies

Ingredients:

- 2¾ cups all-purpose flour
- 1½ teaspoons baking soda
- ½ teaspoon salt
- 12 tablespoons (1½ sticks) unsalted butter, softened
- 1 cup light brown sugar
- 1 cup granulated sugar
- Two eggs, at room temperature
- 2½ teaspoons apple cider vinegar
- 1 tsp. vanilla extract
- 2 cups semisweet chocolate chips
- Eight slices bacon, cooked and crumbled

Directions:

1. In a prepared large bowl, combine the flour, baking soda, and salt, and mix well.
2. In a separate large bowl, using an electric mixer on medium speed, cream the butter and sugars. Reduce the rate to low and mix in the eggs, vinegar, and vanilla.
3. With the mixer speed still on low, slowly incorporate the dry ingredients, chocolate chips, and bacon pieces.
4. Supply your smoker with wood pellets and follow the manufacturer's specific start-up procedure. Preheat, with the lid closed, to 375degrees F (191°C).
5. Line a large baking sheet drop a rounded teaspoonful of cookie batter onto the prepared baking sheet and place on the grill grate. Close the lid and smoke for 10 to 12 minutes, or until the cookies are browned around the edges.

Nutrition: Energy (calories): 376 kcal Protein: 5.88 g Fat: 18.72 g Carbohydrates: 50.08 g

SAUCES AND RUBS

Black Bean Dipping Sauce

Preparation Time: 10 Minutes
Cooking Time: 30 Minutes
Servings: 4
Ingredients:

- 2 tablespoons black bean paste
- 2 tablespoons peanut butter
- 1 tablespoon maple syrup
- 2 tablespoons olive oil

Directions:

1. In a blender place all ingredients and blend until smooth
2. Pour smoothie in a glass and serve

Nutrition: Calories: 20 Carbs: 13g Fat: 1g Protein: 0g

Maple Syrup Dipping Sauce

Preparation Time: 10 Minutes
Cooking Time: 30 Minutes
Servings: 4
Ingredients:

- 2 tablespoons peanut butter
- 2 tablespoons maple syrup
- 2 tsp olive oil
- 2 tablespoon Korean black bean paste

Directions:

1. In a blender place all ingredients and blend until smooth
2. Pour smoothie in a glass and serve

Nutrition: Calories: 60 Carbs: 13g Fat: 1g Protein: 0g

Soy Dipping Sauce

Preparation Time: 10 Minutes
Cooking Time: 30 Minutes
Servings: 4
Ingredients:

- ¼ cup soy sauce
- ¼ cup sugar
- ¼ cup rice vinegar
- ½ cup scallions
- ½ cup cilantro

Directions:

1. smoothie in a glass and serve

Original Ketchup

Preparation Time: 10 minutes
Cooking Time: 20 minutes
Serving: 4
Ingredients

- ½ a cup of chopped pitted dates
- 1 can of 6-ounce tomato paste
- 1 can of 14-ounce diced tomatoes
- 2 tablespoon of coconut vinegar
- ½ a cup of bone broth
- 1 teaspoon of garlic powder
- 1 teaspoon of onion powder
- 1 teaspoon of salt
- ½ a teaspoon of cayenne pepper

Directions:

1. Add the ingredients to a small-sized saucepan
2. Cook on medium-low for 20 minutes
3. Remove the heat
4. Take an immersion blender and blend the mixture until smooth
5. Remove the mixer and simmer on low for 10 minutes
6. Use as needed

Nutrition: Calories: 10 Carbs: 7g Protein: 2g

NUT AND FRUIT RECIPES

Simple Cinnamon Sugar Pumpkin Seeds

Preparation Time: 30 minutes
Cooking Time: 30 minutes
Servings: 8-12
Ingredients:

- 2 tablespoon sugar
- Seeds from a pumpkin
- 1 teaspoon cinnamon
- 2 tablespoon melted butter

Directions:

1. Add blackstones to your smoker and follow your cooker's startup procedure. Preheat your smoker, with your lid closed, until it reaches 350.
2. Clean the seeds and toss them in the melted butter. Add them to the sugar and cinnamon. Spread them out on a baking sheet, place on the grill, and smoke for 25 minutes.
3. Serve.

Nutrition: Calories: 127 cal Protein: 5mg Carbohydrates: 15g Fiber: 0g Fat: 21g

TRADITIONAL RECIPES

Creative Sablefish

Preparation Time: 15 minutes
Cooking Time: 3 hours
Servings: 8
Ingredients:

- 2-3 pounds of sablefish fillets
- 1 cup of kosher salts
- ¼ cup of sugar
- 2 tablespoon of garlic powder
- Honey for glazing
- Sweet paprika for dusting

Directions:

1. Take a bowl and mix salt, garlic powder, and sugar
2. Pour on a healthy layer of your mix into a lidded plastic tub, large enough to hold the fish
3. Cut up the fillet into pieces
4. Gently massage the salt mix into your fish meat and place them with the skin side down on to the salt mix in the plastic tub
5. Cover up the container and keep it in your fridge for as many hours as the fish weighs
6. Remove the sablefish from the tub and place it under cold water for a while
7. Pat, it dries using a kitchen towel and puts it back to the fridge, keep it uncovered overnight
8. Take your drip pan and add water, cover with aluminum foil. Pre-heat your smoker to 225 degrees F
9. Use water fill water pan halfway through and place it over drip pan. Add wood chips to the side tray
10. Smoke for 2-3 hours
11. After the first hour of smoking, make sure to baste the fish with honey and keep repeating this after every hour
12. One done, move the fish to a cooling rack and baste it with honey one last time
13. Let it cool for about an hour
14. Use tweezers to pull out the bone pins
15. Dust the top with some paprika and wait for 30 minutes to let the paprika sink in
16. Put the fish in your fridge
17. Serve hot or chilled!

Nutrition: Calories: 171 Fats: 10g Carbs: 13g Fiber: 1g

SAUCES, RUBS, AND MARINATES

Smoked Thyme Chicken Rub

Preparation Time: 5 minutes
Cooking Time: 5 minutes
Servings: 1
Ingredients:

- 1/4 cup olive oil
- 1/4 cup soy marinade
- 2 tbsp. onion powder
- 2 tbsp. cayenne pepper
- 2 tsp. paprika
- Two garlic cloves, crushed
- 1 to ½ tsp. black pepper
- 1 tsp. dried oregano
- 1 tsp. dried thyme

Directions:

1. Simply place all ingredients into an airtight jar, stir well to combine then close.
2. Use within six months.

Nutrition: Calories: 20 Fat: 1g Carbs: 6g Protein: 1g

RUBS, INJECTABLES, MARINADES, AND MOPS

Lemon Butter Mop for Seafood

Preparation Time: 10 Minutes
Cooking Time: 0 Minutes
Servings: ¼ Cup
Ingredients:

- 8 tablespoons (1 stick) butter
- Juice of 1 small lemon
- 1 tablespoon fine salt
- 1½ teaspoons garlic powder
- 1½ teaspoons dried dill weed

Directions:

1. 1.In a small skillet over medium heat, melt the butter.
2. 2.Stir in the lemon juice, salt, garlic powder, and dill, stirring until well mixed. Use immediately.

Nutrition: Calories: 10 Carbs: 6g Protein: 1g

Tea Injectable

Preparation Time: 10 Minutes
Cooking Time: 0 Minutes
Servings: 2 Cups
Ingredients:
- ¼ cup favorite spice rub or shake
- 2 cups water

Directions:

1. 1.Place the rub in a standard paper coffee filter and tie it up with kitchen string to seal.
2. 2.In a small pot over high heat, bring the water to a boil.
3. 3.Drop the filter into the boiling water and remove the pot from the heat. Let it steep for 30 minutes.
4. 4.Remove and discard the filter. Discard any unused tea after injecting the meat.

Nutrition: Calories: 10 Carbs: 6g Protein: 1g

OTHER RECIPES YOU NEVER THOUGHT ABOUT TO GRILL

Sticky Port and Brown Sugar Ham

Preparation Time: 10 minutes
Cooking Time: 52 HOURS, 20 MINUTES
Servings: 6
Ingredients:
THE MEAT

- 1 leg bone-in ham (12-lbs, 5.4-kgs)
- THE INGREDIENTS
- Olive oil
- Port – 1 cup
- Brown sugar – 1 cup
- Fine breadcrumbs – ½ cup
- Marmalade, fruit of choice – ¼ cup
- THE GRILL
- Soak one bag of hickory wood pellets in water overnight.
- When ready to cook, heat up the pellet grill to 250°F (121°C) and prepare for indirect cooking.

Directions:
1. Hang the pork leg in a cool dry area for up to 2 days.
2. When ready to cook, rub the pork leg with a little olive oil then wrap tightly in aluminum foil and prick a few holes using a fork.
3. Arrange the wrapped ham on a rack in a roasting tin and place it on the grill. Smoke for 2 hours and then unwrap the ham foil from the
    ham.Score the fatty skin in a diamond pattern.
4. Combine the port, sugar, breadcrumbs, and marmalade in a bowl. Spread the mixture evenly over the ham and return to the grill for 1½
    hours basting regularly with leftover glaze.
5. Take the ham off the grill and allow resting for 15 minutes before slicing and serving.

Nutrition: Calories: 501 Protein: 44g Vitamin D: 5mcg 26% Calcium: 122mg 9% Iron: 16mg: 90% Potassium: 625mg:

Mesquite Smoked Duck Legs with Polenta

Preparation Time: 10 minutes
Cooking Time: 5 HOURS, 45 MINUTES
Servings: 4-6
Ingredients:

- THE MEAT
- 6 duck legs   •
- THE MARINADE
- Kosher salt – ¼ cup
- 4 garlic cloves, peeled, ground to a paste
- Shallot, chopped – ¼ cup
- Thyme, chopped – 1 tablespoon
- 1 bay leaf, crushed
- Zest of 1 lemon
- Zest of 1 orange
- THE POLENTA
- Chicken stock – 5 cups
- Coarsely ground polenta – 1 cup
- Kosher salt
- Unsalted butter – 2 tablespoons
- THE MUSHROOMS
- Unsalted butter – 2 tablespoons
- Wild mushrooms, sliced – 3 cups
- Chicken stock – ½ cup
- Salt and black pepper
- Fresh thyme leaves – ½ tablespoon
- THE GRILL
- When you are ready to cook, with the lid open and the grill on smoke establish the fire for 4-5 minutes.
- Set the temperature to 180°F (82°C) and with the lid closed preheat for 12-15 minutes

Directions:

1. In a mixing bowl, combine the salt with the garlic paste, shallot, thyme, bay leaf, lemon zest and orange zest.
2. Cover the duck legs with the salt-zest mixture and transfer to the fridge overnight.
3. Remove the duck legs from the mixture and thoroughly rinse before patting dry.
4. Arrange the duck legs directly on the grate and smoke until the duck shreds easily off the bone, for 4-5 hours.

5.   To prepare the polenta, bring the stock to boil in a pan over moderately high heat.

6.   Then, when the stock is boiling, add the polenta while whisking to eliminate any lumps.

7.   Turn down to simmer and cook until the polenta is al dente. You can add a drop stock if the grain appears too dry—season with salt
        and stir in the butter. Keep the polenta warm.

8.   To cook the mushrooms: Over high heat, in a pan melt the butter.

9.   Add the mushrooms and cook until slightly crispy and gently browned.

10.   Add the chicken stock, salt and pepper, transfer to the grill set at a temperature of 350°F (177°C), and cook for between 20-30 minutes,
        while the legs are resting.

11.   Garnish with thyme and serve.

Nutrition: Calories: 641 Protein: 0.7g Vitamin D: 0mcg Calcium: 19mg Iron: 1mg Potassium: 223mg

Pheasant Remake

Preparation Time: 10 minutes
Cooking Time: 8 HOURS, 30 MINUTES
Servings: 4-8
Ingredients:

- THE MEAT
- 1 breast of pheasant, cut into 8 chunks
- Bacon, thickly sliced (1-lbs, 0.45-gms)
- Teriyaki sauce, store-bought – 1 cup
- Water chestnuts – ½ cup
- THE GRILL
- When you are already set to cook, heat up your smoker to 325°F (163°C)

Directions:

1. First, place the chunks of pheasant into a zip lock bag.
2. Pour in ½ cup of teriyaki sauce, and allow marinating overnight.
3. Cut the slices of bacon in half.
4. On a clean platter lay out half of the bacon strips.
5. Put a water chestnut in the middle of each strip of bacon.
6. Remove the pheasant from the bag shaking off any excess sauce.
7. Place the breast meat on top of the water chestnuts in the middle of each strip of bacon.
8. Carefully wrap the ends of the bacon to cover the water chestnuts and pheasant and using a cocktail stick, secure.
9. Place the bacon-wrapped meat directly on the preheated grill and with the lid closed, cook for approximately 20 minutes, or until the internal temperature reaches 165°F (74°C).
10. Baste with any remaining teriyaki sauce during cooking. It is important, however, not to leave the grill hood open for too long a time.

Nutrition: Calories: 501 Protein: 44g Vitamin D: 5mcg 26% Calcium: 122mg 9% Iron: 16mg: 90% Potassium: 625mg:

Smoked Venison and Wild Boar Protein Bars

Preparation Time: 10 minutes
Cooking Time: 5 HOURS, 20 MINUTES
Servings: 8-12
Ingredients:
THE MEAT

- Ground venison (1-lbs, 0.45-gms)
- Ground wild boar (1-lbs, 0.45-gms)

THE INGREDIENTS

- Celery salt – 2 teaspoons
- Red pepper flakes – 2 teaspoon

•THE GRILL

- When you are ready to cook, with the grill on smoke and the lid open establish the fire for 4-5 minutes.

Directions:
1. First, place the chunks of pheasant into a zip lock bag.
2. In a bowl, combine the venison with the boar, celery salt and red pepper flakes.
3. Using clean hands, form the mixture into bars 2-ins (5-cms) wide by 4-ins (10-cms) long.
4. Arrange the bars directly onto the grill grate and smoke for between 4-5 hours.
5. Remove the bars from the grill and set aside to completely cool before wrapping.

Nutrition: Calories: 321 Total Carbohydrate 15.5g 6% Dietary Fiber: 0.3g 1% Total Sugars 13.5g Protein: 42.2g Vitamin D: 0mcg 0% Calcium: 25mg 2% Iron: 4mg 24% Potassium: 454mg 10%

Roasted Bacon-Wrapped Shrimp

Preparation Time: 3 minutes
Cooking Time: 15 minutes
Servings: 4

Ingredients:

- 16 large shrimp, peeled and veined
- 8 strips bacon
- 1/4 cup melted butter
- 1-teaspoon lemon juice
- 1 clove garlic, minced
- Salt and pepper to taste

Directions:

1. Set your wood pellet grill to smoke while the lid is open.
2. Do this for 5 minutes.
3. Preheat the grill to 450 degrees F.
4. Wrap the shrimp with the bacon slices.
5. Secure with a toothpick.
6. In a bowl, mix the butter, lemon juice, and garlic.
7. Brush the shrimp with this mixture.
8. Roast for 11 minutes.
9. Season with the salt and pepper before serving.
10. Serving Suggestion: Serve with sweet chili sauce.

Tip: You can also smoke the shrimp for 30 minutes before grilling.

Nutrition: Calories: 501Protein: 44g Vitamin D: 5mcg 26% Calcium: 122mg 9% Iron: 16mg: 90% Potassium: 625mg:

Roasted Green Beans

Preparation Time: 5 minutes
Cooking Time: 1 hour
Servings: 6
Ingredients:

- 4 slices bacon
- 2 lb. Green beans trimmed and sliced in half.
- 2 cups chicken broth
- 2 cups of water
- Hickory bacon seasoning
- 1-tablespoon butter

Directions:

1. Turn on your wood pellet grill.
2. Set the temperature to 350 degrees F.
3. Add a cast-iron skillet on top of the grill and preheat.
4. Place the bacon slices in the pan.
5. Cook until golden and crispy.
6. Transfer the bacon to a cutting board. Chop into small pieces.
7. Put the green beans in the pan along with the rest of the ingredients except the butter.
8. Seal the lid.
9. Cook for 1 hour.
10. Add the beans to a bowl.
11. Stir in the butter and bacon bits.
12. Serving Suggestion: given as a side to grilled steak.

Tip: You can also add baby potatoes to this recipe.
Nutrition: Calories: 641 Protein: 0.7g Vitamin D: 0mcg Calcium: 19mg Iron: 1mg Potassium: 223mg

Roasted Prime Rib

Preparation Time: 0 minutes
Cooking Time: 5 minutes
Servings: 8
Ingredients:

- 10 cloves garlic, minced
- 2 lb. prime rib roast
- Salt and pepper to taste
- 2 teaspoons steak seasoning

Directions:

1. Preheat your wood pellet grill.
2. Set the temperature to 400 degrees F.
3. Rub the prime rib with the garlic.
4. Season with the salt, pepper, and steak seasoning.
5. Roast in the wood pellet grill for 50 minutes.
6. Place the prime rib on a cutting board.
7. Let rest for 10 minutes before serving.
8. Serving Suggestion: Garnish with fresh herb sprigs. Serve with grilled asparagus.

Tip: It is also a good idea to cook the prime rib in a baking pan to catch the drippings.
Nutrition: Calories: 501 Protein: 44g Vitamin D: 5mcg 26% Calcium: 122mg 9% Iron: 16mg: 90%

Roasted Mustard Steak

Preparation Time: 10 minutes
Cooking Time: 4 hours
Servings: 8
Ingredients:

- 1-cup mustard
- 2 tablespoon garlic, crushed
- Salt and pepper to taste
- 1 prime rib roast

Directions:

1. In a bowl, mix the mustard, garlic, salt, and pepper.
2. Rub the roast with this mixture.
3. Preheat your wood pellet grill.
4. Set it to 400 degrees F.
5. Add the roast on the grill.
6. Seal the lid.
7. Roast for 45 minutes.
8. Reduce temperature to 325 degrees F.
9. Cook for 2 hours and 30 minutes.
10. Let it stay for 15 minutes before slicing and serving.
11. Serving Suggestion: Serve with mashed potatoes and gravy.

Tip: Use coarse sea salt for the crusty finish.
Nutrition: Calories: 641 Protein: 0.7g Vitamin D: 0mcg Calcium: 19mg Iron: 1mg Potassium: 223mg

Roast Beef Sandwich

Preparation Time: 15 minutes
Cooking Time: 8 hours and 30 minutes
Servings: 10
Ingredients:

- 5 lb. beef chuck roast, trimmed
- 4 cups beef broth
- 2 tablespoons sweet, spicy rub
- 1 can green chili, chopped
- 7 oz. jarred salsa Verde
- 1-pack slider buns
- Cheddar cheese, sliced

Directions:

1. Start your wood pellet grill.
2. Set it to 300 degrees F.
3. Put the roast on a baking pan.
4. Pour the broth on top of the roast.
5. Sprinkle all sides with the sweet-spicy rub.
6. Add the chili and salsa on top.
7. Wrap the roast with foil.
8. Roast for 6 hours.
9. Let rest for 30 minutes on a cutting board.
10. Shred the beef using a fork.
11. Stuff the shredded beef into the slider buns with the cheese.

Nutrition: Calories: 501 Protein: 44g Vitamin D: 5mcg 26% Calcium: 122mg 9% Iron: 16mg: 90% Potassium: 625mg

Smoked Ham

Preparation Time: 10 minute
Cooking Time: 2 hours and 30 minutes
Servings: 8
Ingredients:

- 1 lb. bacon
- 2 apples, sliced
- 1 spiral cut smoked ham
- Applewood bacon dry rub
- 2 tablespoons butter
- 5 tablespoons mustard
- 3 tablespoons apple cider vinegar
- 1-1/2 cup apple cider
- 2 tablespoons cornstarch
- 1/2 cup pure maple syrup

Directions:

1. Set your wood pellet grill to smoke.
2. Set the temperature to 250 degrees F.
3. Smoke the bacon for 20 minutes, flipping once or twice.
4. Reduce temperature to 225 degrees F.
5. Put the ham in a roasting pan.
6. Slice the ham but not all the way through.
7. Insert apples and bacon into the slices.
8. Sprinkle all sides of the pan with the dry rub.
9. Roast the ham for 1 hour.
10. In a pan over medium heat, mix the rest of the ingredients. Bring to a boil.
11. Reduce heat and simmer for 15 minutes.
12. Brush the ham with this mixture.
13. Let rest for 20 minutes.
14. Serve with the remaining sauce.

Tip: Use a cast iron roasting pan for this recipe.
Nutrition: Calories: 641 Protein: 0.7g Vitamin D: 0mcg Calcium: 19mg Iron: 1mg Potassium: 223mg

Roasted Beer Chicken

Preparation Time: 15 minutes
Cooking Time: 2 hours and 30 minutes
Servings: 4
Ingredients:

- 1 whole chicken
- Lemon garlic seasoning
- 1 can beer

Directions:

1. Preheat your wood pellet grill to 400 degrees F.
2. Sprinkle the chicken with the lemon garlic seasoning.
3. Place the chicken in a roasting pan.
4. Pour the beer into the pan.
5. Add the pan to the grill and roast for 2 hours.
6. Serving Suggestion: Serve with steamed vegetables.

Tip: Internal temperature of the chicken should reach 165 degrees F.
Nutrition: Calories: 501 Protein: 44g Vitamin D: 5mcg 26% Calcium: 122mg 9% Iron: 16mg: 90% Potassium: 625mg

Braised Pork Belly

Preparation Time: 15 minutes
Cooking Time: 1 hour and 45 minutes
Servings: 4
Ingredients:

- 2 lb. pork belly, sliced into cubes
- 1 onion, sliced thinly
- 2 cloves garlic, crushed
- 1 teaspoon minced ginger
- 1 beer
- 3 cups beef broth
- 2 tablespoons soy sauce
- 2 tablespoons of rice wine vinegar
- 1-tablespoon cooking wine
- 3 tablespoons sugar
- 1-teaspoon C

Directions:

1. Put a Dutch oven over medium-high heat.
2. Cook the pork belly until brown.
3. Stir in the onion, garlic, and ginger.
4. Put and mix the rest to the pan. Bring to a boil.
5. Turn off the stove.
6. Start your wood pellet grill.
7. Set it to 325 degrees F.
8. Place the pan on top of the grill.
9. Braise for 1 hour and 30 minutes.
10. Serving Suggestion: Serve with noodles or white rice.

Tip: You can also smoke the pork belly for 15 minutes before braising.
Nutrition: Calories: 641 Protein: 0.7g Vitamin D: 0mcg Calcium: 19mg Iron: 1mg Potassium: 223

CONCLUSION

I n conclusion, it is a fact that the Blackstone pellet grill has made grilling easier and better for humanity, and Grilling, which is part of the so-called "dietetic" cooking, had been made easier through the Blackstone grill. Giving us that tasty meal, we've been craving for and thus improving the quality of life. This book made you a lot of recipes that you can make at your home with your new Blackstone Pellet grill. The recipes will give so much satisfaction with the tenderness and tasty BBQ.

The Blackstone barbecues are electrical, and a typical 3-position function controls them. A cylindrical device transmits the pellets from the storage to the fire place, like a pellet stove. Blackstone Grill smoker promotes an excellent outcome for your meat and other recipes. This smoker provides a tasty for your foods. To achieve such a real taste, you need the quality of materials and get the exact smoking. It is best if you get the maximum consistency of smoking so that you can have the best result of your meat and other recipes. Moreover, if you add more flavors to your recipes, use the best wood pellet for cooking for your food.

Many people ask me questions on why I chose Blackstone pellet grill, and you might think, well, the answer is clear and true, and yes! It's right before us. Why?

It cooks with a wood fire, giving an excellent quality in taste because nothing is like it: real wood, real smoking, natural aroma. In terms of the cooking process, it has changed a lot. Experts chefs tend to have new experiments with new flavor and ingredients to create a delicious and tasty recipe.

Grilling is one of the most popular cooking processes that grant a perfect taste to your recipes. Grilling is a much healthier method than others because its benefits food, preserves flavor, and nutrients. But from the other side, a Blackstone grill smoker's wood pellet grill allows you

to grill your food quickly and with less effort and smoke. The advantage of having a Blackstone grill smoker in your home is the versatility, helps you cook food faster, provides a monitoring scale for the temperature,and it is one of the essential parts of cooking.

It is a versatile barbecue. In fact, it can be grilled, smoked, baked, roasted, and stewed—everything you can imagine cooking with the Blackstone grill smoker. You will find that this Blackstone grill smoker is aflexible tool that has a good service.

As we all could testify that using the pellet grill has been made simple by Blackstone: its intuitive control panel has a power button and a knobthat allows you to adjust the temperature comfortably.

Finally, we need to note that through Grilling, we can always find new flavors in our dishes: with Blackstone pellets, you can smoke your dishes, giving them an ever new and different flavor. Blackstone Grill smoker isthe answer you are looking for your taste buds. Don't waste your time and have your own smoker at home and start cooking your favorite recipes with this book.

THE ULTIMATE BLACKSTONE OUTDOOR GAS GRIDDLE COOKBOOK:

Tips and Tricks to master Your Grilling Skills. 100 Tasty and Mouth-Watering Recipeswith Step-by-Step Smoking instructions.

Mark Franklin

GRILL BEEF RECIPES

Wood Pellet Smoked Beef Jerky

Preparation Time: 15 Minutes
Cooking Time: 5 Hours
Servings: 10

Ingredients:

- 3 lb. sirloin steaks, sliced into 1/4-inch thickness
- 2 cups soy sauce
- 1/2 cup brown sugar
- 1 cup pineapple juice
- 2 tbsp sriracha
- 2 tbsp red pepper flake
- 2 tbsp hoisin
- 2 tbsp onion powder
- 2 tbsp rice wine vinegar
- 2 tbsp garlic, minced

Directions:

1. Mix all the fixings in a Ziplock bag.
2. Seal the bag and mix until the beef is well coated.
3. Put the bag in the fridge overnight to let marinate. Remove the bag from the fridge 1 hour before cooking.
4. Startup your wood pallet grill and set it to smoke setting. You need to layout the meat on the grill with a half-inch space between them.
5. Let them cook for 5 hours while turning after every 2-1/2 hours.
6. Transfer from the grill and let cool for 30 minutes before serving.
7. Enjoy.

Nutrition: Calories 80 Total fat 1g Total carbs 5g Protein 14g Sugar 5g Sodium: 650mg

Reverse Seared Flank Steak

Preparation Time: 10 Minutes
Cooking Time: 10 Minutes
Servings: 2
Ingredients:

- 1.5 lb. Flanks steak
- 1 tbsp salt
- 1/2 onion powder
- 1/4 tbsp garlic powder
- 1/2 black pepper, coarsely ground

Directions:

1. Preheat your wood pellet grill to 225°F.
2. In a mixing bowl, mix salt, onion powder, garlic powder, and pepper. Generously rub the steak with the mixture.
3. Place the steaks on the preheated grill, close the lid, and let the steak cook.
4. Crank up the grill to high, then let it heat. The steak should be off the grill and tented with foil to keep it warm.
5. Once the grill is heated up to 450°F, place the steak back and grill for 3 minutes per side.
6. Remove from heat, pat with butter, and serve. Enjoy.

Nutrition: Calories 112 Total fat 5g Total carbs 1g Protein 16g Sodium: 737mg

Smoked Midnight Brisket

Preparation Time: 15 Minutes
Cooking Time: 12 Minutes
Servings: 6
Ingredients:

- 1 tbsp Worcestershire sauce
- 1 tbsp Blackstone beef Rub
- 1 tbsp Blackstone Chicken rub
- 1 tbsp Blackstone Blackened Saskatchewan rub
- 5 lb. flat cut brisket
- 1 cup beef broth

Directions:

1. Rub the sauce and rubs in a mixing bowl, then rub the mixture on the meat.
2. Preheat your grill to 180°**F** with the lid closed for 15 minutes. You can use super smoke if you desire.
3. Place the meat on the grill and grill for 6 hours or until the internal temperature reaches 160°**F**.
4. Remove the meat from the grill and double wrap it with foil.
5. Add beef broth and return to grill, with the temperature increased to 225°F. Cook for 4 hours or until the internal temperature reaches 204°F.
6. Remove from grill and let rest for 30 minutes. Serve and enjoy with your favorite BBQ sauce.

Nutrition: Calories 200 Total fat 14g Total carbs 3g Protein 14g Sodium: 680mg

Cocoa Crusted Grilled Flank Steak

Preparation Time: 15 Minutes
Cooking Time: 6 Minutes
Servings: 7
Ingredients:

- 1 tbsp cocoa powder
- 2 tbsp chili powder
- 1 tbsp chipotle chili powder
- 1/2 tbsp garlic powder
- 1/2 tbsp onion powder
- 1-1/2 tbsp brown sugar
- 1 tbsp cumin
- 1 tbsp smoked paprika
- 1 tbsp kosher salt
- 1/2 tbsp black pepper
- Olive oil
- 4 lb. Flank steak

Directions:

1. Whisk together cocoa, chili powder, garlic powder, onion powder, sugar, cumin, paprika, salt, and pepper in a mixing bowl.
2. Drizzle the steak with oil, then rub with the cocoa mixture on both sides.
3. Preheat your wood pellet grill for 15 minutes with the lid closed.
4. Cook the meat on the grill grate for 5 minutes or until the internal temperature reaches 135°F.
5. Remove the meat from the grill and cool for 15 minutes to allow the juices to redistribute.
6. Slice the meat against the grain and on a sharp diagonal.
7. Serve and enjoy.

Nutrition: Calories 420 Total fat 26g Total carbs 21g Protein 3g Sugar 7g, Fiber 8g Sodium: 2410mg

Wood Pellet Grill Prime Rib Roast

Preparation Time: 5 Minutes
Cooking Time: 4 Hours
Servings: 10
Ingredients:

- 7 lb. bone prime rib roast
- Blackstone prime rib rub

Directions:

1. Coat the roast generously with the rub, then wrap in a plastic wrap. Let sit in the fridge for 24 hours to marinate.
2. Set the temperatures to 500°F.to to preheat with the lid closed for 15 minutes.
3. Place the rib directly on the grill fat side up and cook for 30 minutes.
4. Decrease the temperature to 300°F and cook for 4 hours or until the internal temperature is 120°F- rare, 130°F-medium rare, 140°F-medium and 150°F-well done.
5. Remove from the grill and let rest for 30 minutes, then serve and enjoy.

Nutrition: Calories 290 Total fat 23g Total carbs 0g Protein 19g Sodium: 54mg Potassium 275mg

Smoked Longhorn Cowboy Tri-Tip

Preparation Time: 15 Minutes
Cooking Time: 4 Hours
Servings: 7
Ingredients:

- 3 lb. tri-tip roast
- 1/8 cup coffee, ground
- 1/4 cup Blackstone beef rub

Directions:

1. Preheat the grill to 180°F with the lid closed for 15 minutes.
2. Meanwhile, rub the roast with coffee and beef rub. Place the roast on the grill grate and smoke for 3 hours.
3. Remove the roast from the grill and double wrap it with foil. Increase the temperature to 275°F.
4. Return the meat to the grill and cook for 90 minutes or until the internal temperature reaches 135°F.
5. Remove from the grill, unwrap it and let rest for 10 minutes before serving.
6. Enjoy.

Nutrition: Calories 245 Total fat 14g Total Carbs 0g Protein 23g Sodium: 80mg

Wood Pellet Grill Teriyaki Beef Jerky

Preparation Time: 15 Minutes
Cooking Time: 5 Hours
Servings: 10
  Ingredients:

- 3 cups soy sauce
- 2 cups brown sugar
- Three garlic cloves
- 2-inch ginger knob, peeled and chopped
- 1 tbsp sesame oil
- 4 lb. beef, skirt steak

Directions:

1. Place all the fixings except the meat in a food processor. Pulse until well mixed.
2. Trim any extra fat from the meat and slice into 1/4-inch slices. Add the steak with the marinade into a zip lock bag and let marinate for 12-24 hours in a fridge.
3. Set the wood pellet grill to smoke and let preheat for 5 minutes.
4. Arrange the steaks on the grill, leaving a space between each. Let smoke for 5 hours.
5. Remove the steak from the grill and serve when warm.

Nutrition: Calories 80 Total fat 1g Total Carbs 7g Protein 11g Sugar 6g Sodium: 390mg

Grilled Butter Basted Rib-eye

Preparation Time: 20 Minutes
Cooking Time: 20 Minutes
Servings: 4
Ingredients:

- Two rib-eye steaks, bone-in
- Salt to taste
- Pepper to taste
- 4 tbsp butter, unsalted

Directions:

1. Mix steak, salt, and pepper in a Ziplock bag. Seal the bag and mix until the beef is well coated. Ensure you get as much air as possible from the Ziplock bag.
2. Set the wood pellet grill temperature to high with a closed lid for 15 minutes. Place a cast-iron into the grill.
3. Place the steaks on the grill's hottest spot and cook for 5 minutes with the lid closed.
4. Open the lid and add butter to the skillet. When it's almost melted, place the steak on the skillet with the grilled side up.
5. Cook for 5 minutes while busting the meat with butter. Close the lid and cook until the temperature is 130°**F.**
6. Remove the steak from the skillet and let rest for 10 minutes before enjoying with the reserved butter.

Nutrition: Calories 745 Total fat 65g Total Carbs 5g Net Carbs 5g Protein 35g

Wood Pellet Smoked Ribeye Steaks

Preparation Time: 15 Minutes
Cooking Time: 35 Minutes
Servings: 1
   Ingredients:

- 2-inch thick ribeye steaks
- Steak rub of choice

Directions:

1. Preheat your pellet grill to low smoke.
2. Sprinkle the steak with your favorite steak rub and place it on the grill. Let it smoke for 25 minutes.
3. Remove the steak from the grill and set the temperature to 400°**F.**
4. Return the steak to the grill and sear it for 5 minutes on each side.
5. Cook until the desired temperature is achieved; 125°F-rare, 145°F-Medium, and 165°F.-Well done.
6. Wrap the steak with foil and let rest for 10 minutes before serving. Enjoy.

Nutrition: Calories 225 Total fat 10.4g Total Carbs 0.2g Protein 32.5g Sodium: 63mg, Potassium 463mg

Smoked Trip Tip with Java Chophouse

Preparation Time: 10 Minutes
Cooking Time: 90 Minutes
Servings: 4
Ingredients:

- 2 tbsp olive oil
- 2 tbsp java chophouse seasoning
- 3 lb. trip tip roast, fat cap, and silver skin removed

Directions:

1. Startup your wood pellet grill and smoker and set the temperature to 225°F.
2. Rub the roast with olive oil and seasoning, then place it on the smoker rack.
3. Smoke until the internal temperature is 140°F.
4. Remove the tri-tip from the smoker and let rest for 10 minutes before serving. Enjoy.

Nutrition: Calories 270 Total fat 7g Total Carbs 0g Protein 23g Sodium: 47mg Potassium 289mg

Supper Beef Roast

Preparation Time: 5 Minutes
Cooking Time: 3 Hours
Servings: 7
Ingredients:

- 3-1/2 beef top round
- 3 tbsp vegetable oil
- Prime rib rub
- 2 cups beef broth
- One russet potato, peeled and sliced
- Two carrots, peeled and sliced
- Two celery stalks, chopped
- One onion, sliced
- Two thyme sprigs

Directions:

1. Rub the roast with vegetable oil and place it on the roasting fat side up. Season with prime rib rub, then pours the beef broth.
2. Set the temperature to 500°F and preheat the wood pellet grill for 15 minutes with the lid closed.
3. Cook for 30 minutes or until the roast is well seared.
4. Reduce temperature to 225°F. Add the veggies and thyme and cover with foil. Cook for three more hours or until the internal temperature reaches 135°F.
5. Remove from the grill and let rest for 10 minutes. Slice against the grain and serve with vegetables and the pan drippings.
6. Enjoy.

Nutrition: Calories 697 Total fat 10g Total Carbs 127g Protein 34g Sugar 14g Fiber 22g Sodium: 3466mg Potassium 2329mg

Wood Pellet Grill Deli-Style Roast Beef

Preparation Time: 15 Minutes
Cooking Time: 4 Hours
Servings: 2
Ingredients:

- 4lb round-bottomed roast
- 1 tbsp coconut oil
- 1/4 tbsp garlic powder
- 1/4 tbsp onion powder
- 1/4 tbsp thyme
- 1/4 tbsp oregano
- 1/2 tbsp paprika
- 1/2 tbsp salt
- 1/2 tbsp black pepper

Directions:

1. Combine all the dry hubs to get a dry rub.
2. Roll the roast in oil, then coat with the rub.
3. Set your grill to 185°F and place the roast on the grill.
4. Smoke for 4 hours or until the internal temperature reaches 140°F.
5. Remove the roast from the grill and let rest for 10 minutes.
6. Slice thinly and serve.

Nutrition: Calories 90 Total fat 3g Total Carbs 0g Protein 14g Sodium: 420mg

GRILL PORK RECIPES

Plum Flavored Glazed Pork Belly Kebabs

Preparation Time: 10-15 minutes

Cooking Time: 4 hours 30 minutes

Serving: 4

Ingredients:

- 1-pound pork belly
- ½ cup Asia plum sauce
- 2 teaspoons Asian chili paste
- 1 tablespoon soy sauce
- 2 garlic clove, minced
- Salt to taste
- Pepper to taste
- 8 skewers

Directions:

1. Cut pork belly into cubes of 1-inch thickness, thread onto skewers, and season with salt and pepper
2. Make plum glaze by taking a medium-sized bowl and adding Asian plum sauce, chili paste, soy sauce, garlic, and mix
3. Take your drip pan and add water; cover with aluminum foil. Pre-heat your smoker to 250 degrees F
4. Use water fill water pan halfway through and place it over drip pan. Add wood chips to the side tray
5. Place kebab threaded skewers on the grid and cook for 3-4 hours' minutes, making sure to turn occasionally
6. Make sure to baste for just 10 minutes before cooking completes; make sure not to burn it
7. Once turn, remove from grill and serve
8. Enjoy!

Nutrition: Calories: 135 Fat: 9g Carbohydrates: 5g Protein: 17g

Maple Baby Backs

Preparation Time: 25 minutesCooking Time: 4 hours Servings: 4-6

Ingredients:

- 2 (2- or 3-pound) racks baby back ribs
- 2 tablespoons yellow mustard
- 1 batch Sweet Brown Sugar Rub
- ½ cup plus 2 tablespoons maple syrup, divided
- 2 tablespoons light brown sugar
- 1 cup Pepsi or other non-diet cola
- ¼ cup Bill's Best BBQ Sauce

Directions:

1. Supply your smoker with wood pellets and follow the manufacturer's specific start-up procedure. Preheat the grill
2. Eradicate the membrane. This can be done by cutting just through the membrane in an X pattern and working a paper towel between the membrane and the ribs to pull it off.
3. Coat the ribs on both sides with mustard and season them with the rub. Rub into meat.
4. Grill ribs and smoke for 3 hours.
5. Remove grill and place bone-side up, on enough aluminum foil to wrap the ribs completely. Add maple syrup over the ribs and sprinkle them with 1 tablespoon of brown sugar. Flip the ribs and repeat the maple syrup and brown sugar application on the meat side.
6. Increase the grill's temperature to 300°F.
7. Fold in three sides of the foil around the ribs and add the cola. Fold in the last side, completely enclosing the ribs and liquid. Place ribs back to the grill for 30 to 45 minutes.
8. Remove the ribs from the grill and unwrap them from the foil.
9. In a small bowl, stir together the barbecue sauce and remaining 6 tablespoons of maple syrup. Use this to baste the ribs. Return the ribs to the grill, without the foil, and cook for 15 minutes to caramelize the sauce.
10. Cut into individual ribs and serve immediately.

Nutrition: Calories: 330 CalFat: 24 g Carbohydrates: 11 g Protein: 17 gFiber: 0 g

Simple Smoked Baby Backs

Preparation Time: 25 minutes
Cooking Time: 4-6 hours
Servings: 4-8
Ingredients:

- 2 (2- or 3-pound) racks baby back ribs
- 2 tablespoons yellow mustard
- 1 batch Not-Just-for-Pork Rub

Directions:

1. Supply your smoker with wood pellets and follow the manufacturer's specific start-up procedure. Preheat grill
2. Eradicate the membrane from the backside of the ribs. This can be done by cutting just through the membrane in an X pattern and working a paper towel between the membrane and the ribs to pull it off.
3. Coat the ribs on both sides with mustard and season them with the rub. Work rubs onto meat.
4. smoke until their internal temperature reaches between 190°F and 200°F.
5. Remove the racks from the grill and cut into individual ribs. Serve immediately.

Nutrition: Calories: 245 Cal Fat: 12 g Carbohydrates: 10 g Protein: 22 g Fiber: 0 g

Sweet Smoked Country Ribs

Preparation Time: 25 minutesCooking Time: 4hours Servings: 2-4

Ingredients:

- 2 pounds country-style ribs
- 1 batch Sweet Brown Sugar Rub
- 2 tablespoons light brown sugar
- 1 cup Pepsi or other cola
- ¼ cup Bill's Best BBQ Sauce

Directions:

1. Supply your smoker with wood pellets and follow the manufacturer's specific start-up procedure. With the lid closed, preheat the grill until the temperature is 180 degrees
2. Sprinkle the ribs with the rub and use your hands to work the rub into the meat.
3. Place the ribs directly on the grill grate and smoke for 3 hours.
4. Remove the ribs from the grill and place them on enough aluminum foil to wrap them completely. Dust the brown sugar over the ribs.
5. Increase the grill's temperature to 300°F.
6. Fold in three sides of the foil around the ribs and add the cola. Fold in the last side, completely enclosing the ribs and liquid. Return the ribs to the grill and cook for 45 minutes.
7. Remove the ribs from the foil and place them on the grill grate. Baste all sides of the ribs with barbecue sauce. Cook for 15 minutes more to caramelize the sauce.
8. Remove the ribs from the grill and serve immediately.

Nutrition: Calories: 230 Cal Fat: 17 g Carbohydrates: 0 g Protein: 20 g Fiber: 0 g

Classic Pulled Pork

Preparation Time: 15 minutes
Cooking Time: 16-20 hours
Servings: 8-12
Ingredients:

- 1 (6- to 8-pound) bone-in pork shoulder
- 2 tablespoons yellow mustard
- 1 batch Not-Just-for-Pork Rub

Directions:

1. Supply your smoker with wood pellets and follow the manufacturer's specific start-up procedure.
2. Coat the pork shoulder all over with mustard and season it with the rub.
3. Place the shoulder on the grill grate and smoke until its internal temperature reaches 195°F.
4. Pull the shoulder from the grill and wrap it completely in aluminum foil or butcher paper. Place it in a cooler, cover the cooler, and let it rest for 1 or 2 hours.
5. Remove the pork shoulder from the cooler and unwrap it. Remove the shoulder bone and pull the pork apart using just your fingers. Serve immediately as desired. Leftovers are encouraged.

Nutrition: Calories: 414 Cal Fat: 29 g Carbohydrates: 1 g Protein: 38 g Fiber: 0 g

Maple-Smoked Pork Chops

Preparation Time: 10 minutes
Cooking Time: 55 minutes
Servings: 4

Ingredients:

- 4 (8-ounce) pork chops, bone-in or boneless (I use boneless)
- Salt
- Freshly ground black pepper

Directions:

1. Supply your smoker with wood pellets and follow the manufacturer's specific start-up procedure.
2. Drizzle pork chop with salt and pepper to season.
3. Place the chops directly on the grill grate and smoke for 30 minutes.
4. Increase the grill's temperature to 350°F. Continue to cook the chops until their internal temperature reaches 145°F.
5. Remove the pork chops from the grill and let them rest for 5 minutes before serving.

Nutrition: Calories: 130 Cal Fat: 12 g Carbohydrates: 3 g Protein: 20 g Fiber: 0 g

Apple-Smoked Pork Tenderloin

Preparation Time: 15 minutes
Cooking Time: 4-5 hours
Servings: 4-6
Ingredients:

- 2 (1-pound) pork tenderloins
- 1 batch Not-Just-for-Pork Rub

Directions:

1. Supply your smoker with wood pellets and follow the manufacturer's specific start-up procedure. Preheat the grill
2. Generously season the tenderloins with the rub. W
3. Put tenderloins on the grill and smoke for 4 or 5 hours, until their internal temperature reaches 145°F.
4. The tenderloins must be put out of the grill and let it rest for 5-10 minutes then begin slicing into thin pieces before serving

Nutrition: Calories: 180 Cal Fat: 8 g Carbohydrates: 3 g Protein: 24 g Fiber: 0 g

Barbecued Tenderloin

Preparation Time: 5 minutesCooking Time:
30 minutes Servings: 4-6

Ingredients:

- 2 (1-pound) pork tenderloins
- 1 batch Sweet and Spicy Cinnamon Rub

Directions:

1. Supply your smoker with wood pellets and follow the manufacturer's specific start-up procedure. Preheat the grill
2. Generously season the tenderloins with the rub. Work rubs onto meat.
3. Place the tenderloins and smoke internal temperature reaches 145°F.
4. As you put out the tenderloins from the grill, let it cool down for 5-10 minutes before slicing it up and serving it

Nutrition: Calories: 186 Cal Fat: 4 g Carbohydrates: 8 g Protein: 29 g Fiber: 1 g

Lovable Pork Belly

Preparation Time: 15 Minutes
Cooking Time: 4 Hours and 30 Minutes
Servings: 4
Ingredients:

- 5 pounds of pork belly
- 1 cup dry rub
- Three tablespoons olive oil

For Sauce

- Two tablespoons honey
- Three tablespoons butter
- 1 cup BBQ sauce

Directions:

1. Take your drip pan and add water. Cover with aluminum foil.
2. Pre-heat your smoker to 250 degrees F
3. Add pork cubes, dry rub, olive oil into a bowl and mix well
4. Use water fill water pan halfway through and place it over drip pan.
5. Add wood chips to the side tray
6. Transfer pork cubes to your smoker and smoke for 3 hours (covered)
7. Remove pork cubes from the smoker and transfer to foil pan, add honey, butter, BBQ sauce, and stir
8. Cover the pan with foil and move back to a smoker, smoke for 90 minutes more
9. Remove foil and smoke for 15 minutes more until the sauce thickens
10. Serve and enjoy!

Nutrition: Calories: 1164 Fat: 68g Carbohydrates: 12g Protein: 104g

County Ribs

Preparation Time: 15 Minutes
Cooking Time: 3 Hours
Servings: 4

Ingredients:

- 4 pounds country-style ribs
- Pork rub to taste
- 2 cups apple juice
- ½ stick butter, melted
- 18 ounces BBQ sauce

Directions:

1. Take your drip pan and add water. Cover with aluminum foil.
2. Pre-heat your smoker to 275 degrees F
3. Season country style ribs from all sides
4. Use water fill water pan halfway through and place it over drip pan.
5. Add wood chips to the side tray.
6. Transfer the ribs to your smoker and smoke for 1 hour and 15 minutes until the internal temperature reaches 160 degrees F
7. Take foil pan and mix melted butter, apple juice, 15 ounces BBQ sauce and put ribs back in the pan, cover with foil
8. Transfer back to smoker and smoke for 1 hour 15 minutes more until the internal temperature reaches 195 degrees F
9. Take ribs out from liquid and place them on racks, glaze ribs with more BBQ sauce, and smoke for 10 minutes more
10. Take them out and let them rest for 10 minutes, serve and enjoy!

Nutrition: Calories: 251 Fat: 25g Carbohydrates: 35g Protein: 76g

Wow-Pork Tenderloin

Preparation Time: 15 Minutes
Cooking Time: 3 Hours
Servings: 4
Ingredients:

- One pork tenderloin
- ¼ cup BBQ sauce
- Three tablespoons dry rub

Directions:

1. Take your drip pan and add water. Cover with aluminum foil.
2. Pre-heat your smoker to 225 degrees F
3. Rub the spice blend all finished the pork tenderloin
4. Use water fill water pan halfway through and place it over drip pan.
5. Add wood chips to the side tray
6. Transfer pork meat to your smoker and smoke for 3 hours until the internal temperature reaches 145 degrees F
7. Brush the BBQ sauce over pork and let it rest
8. Serve and enjoy!

Nutrition: Calories: 405 Fat: 9g Carbohydrates: 15g Protein: 59g

Awesome Pork Shoulder

Preparation Time: 15 Minutes + 24 Hours

Cooking Time: 12 Hours

Servings: 4

Ingredients:

- 8 pounds of pork shoulder

For Rub

- One teaspoon dry mustard
- One teaspoon black pepper
- One teaspoon cumin
- One teaspoon oregano
- One teaspoon cayenne pepper
- 1/3 cup salt
- ¼ cup garlic powder
- ½ cup paprika
- 1/3 cup brown sugar
- 2/3 cup sugar

Directions:

1. Bring your pork under salted water for 18 hours
2. Pull the pork out from the brine and let it sit for 1 hour
3. Rub mustard all over the pork
4. Take a bowl and mix all rub ingredients. Rub mixture all over the meat
5. Wrap meat and leave it overnight
6. Take your drip pan and add water. Cover with aluminum foil. Pre-heat your smoker to 250 degrees F
7. Use water fill water pan halfway through and place it over drip pan. Add wood chips to the side tray.
8. Transfer meat to smoker and smoke for 6 hours
9. Take the pork out and wrap in foil, smoke for 6 hours more at 195 degrees F
10. Shred and serve
11. Enjoy!

Nutrition: Calories: 965 Fat: 65g Carbohydrates: 19g Protein: 71g

Herbed Prime Rib

Preparation Time: 15 Minutes
Cooking Time: 4 Hours
Servings: 4
Ingredients:

- 5 pounds prime rib
- Two tablespoons black pepper
- ¼ cup olive oil
- Two tablespoons salt

Herb Paste

- ¼ cup olive oil
- One tablespoon fresh sage
- One tablespoon fresh thyme
- One tablespoon fresh rosemary
- Three garlic cloves

Directions:

1. Take a blender and add herbs, blend until thoroughly combined
2. Take your drip pan and add water. Cover with aluminum foil.
3. Pre-heat your smoker to 225 degrees F
4. Use water fill water pan halfway through and place it over drip pan.
5. Add wood chips to the side tray
6. Coat rib with olive oil and season it well with salt and pepper
7. Transfer seasoned rib to your smoker and smoke for 4 hours
8. Remove rib from the smoker and keep it on the side. Let it cool for 30 minutes
9. Cut into slices and serve
10. Enjoy!

Nutrition: Calories: 936 Fat: 81g Carbohydrates: 2g Protein: 46g

Premium Sausage Hash

Preparation Time: 30 Minutes
Cooking Time: 45 Minutes
Servings: 4
Ingredients:

- Nonstick cooking spray
- Two finely minced garlic cloves
- One teaspoon basil, dried
- One teaspoon oregano, dried
- One teaspoon onion powder
- One teaspoon of salt
- 4-6 cooked smoker Italian Sausage (Sliced)
- One large-sized bell pepper, diced
- One large onion, diced
- Three potatoes, cut into 1-inch cubes
- Three tablespoons of olive oil
- French bread for serving

Directions:

1. Pre-heat your smoker to 225 degrees Fahrenheit using your desired wood chips
2. Cover the smoker grill rack with foil and coat with cooking spray
3. Take a small bowl and add garlic, oregano, basil, onion powder, and season the mix with salt and pepper
4. Take a large bowl and add sausage slices, bell pepper, potatoes, onion, olive oil, and spice mix
5. Mix well and spread the mixture on your foil-covered rack
6. Place the rack in your smoker and smoke for 45 minutes
7. Serve with your French bread
8. Enjoy!

Nutrition: Calories: 193 Fats: 10g Carbs: 15g Fiber: 2g

Explosive Smoky Bacon

Preparation Time: 20 Minutes
Cooking Time: 2 Hours and 10 Minutes
Servings: 10
Ingredients:

- 1 pound thick-cut bacon
- One tablespoon BBQ spice rub
- 2 pounds bulk pork sausage
- 1 cup cheddar cheese, shredded
- Four garlic cloves, minced
- 18 ounces BBQ sauce

Directions:

1. Take your drip pan and add water; cover with aluminum foil.
2. Pre-heat your smoker to 225 degrees F
3. Use water fill water pan halfway through and place it over drip pan.
4. Add wood chips to the side tray
5. Reserve about ½ a pound of your bacon for cooking later on
6. Lay 2 strips of your remaining bacon on a clean surface in an X formation
7. Alternate the horizontal and vertical bacon strips by waving them tightly in an over and under to create a lattice-like pattern
8. Sprinkle one teaspoon of BBQ rub over the woven bacon
9. Arrange ½ a pound of your bacon in a large-sized skillet and cook them for 10 minutes over medium-high heat
10. Drain the cooked slices on a kitchen towel and crumble them
11. Place your sausages in a large-sized re-sealable bag
12. While the sausages are still in the bag, roll them out to a square that has the same sized as the woven bacon
13. Cut off the bag from the sausage and arrange them sausage over the woven bacon
14. Toss away the bag
15. Sprinkle some crumbled bacon, green onions, cheddar cheese, and garlic over the rolled sausages
16. Pour about ¾ bottle of your BBQ sauce over the sausage and season with some more BBQ rub
17. Roll up the woven bacon tightly all around the sausage, forming a loaf
18. Cook the bacon-sausage loaf in your smoker for about one and a ½ hour
19. Brush up the woven bacon with remaining BBQ sauce and keep smoking for about 30 minutes until the center of the loaf is no longer pink
20. Use an instant thermometer to check if the internal temperature is at least 165 degrees Fahrenheit
21. If yes, then take it out and let it rest for 30 minutes
22. Slice and serve!

Nutrition: Calories: 507 Fats: 36g Carbs: 20g Fiber: 2g

Alabama Pulled Pig Pork

Preparation Time: 1 Hour
Cooking Time: 12 Hours
Servings: 8
Ingredients:

- 2 cups of soy sauce
- 1 cup of Worcestershire sauce
- 1 cup of cranberry grape juice
- 1 cup of teriyaki sauce
- One tablespoon of hot pepper sauce
- Two tablespoons of steak sauce
- 1 cup of light brown sugar
- ½ a teaspoon of ground black pepper
- 2 pound of flank steak cut up into ¼ inch slices

Directions:

1. Take a non-reactive saucepan and add cider, salt, vinegar, brown sugar, cayenne pepper, black pepper, and butter
2. Bring the mix to a boil over medium-high heat
3. Add in water and return the mixture to a boil
4. Carefully rub the pork with the sauce
5. Take your drip pan and add water. Cover with aluminum foil.
6. Pre-heat your smoker to 225 degrees F
7. Use water fill water pan halfway through and place it over drip pan.
8. Add wood chips to the side tray
9. Smoke meat for about 6-10 hours. Make sure to keep basting it with the sauce every hour or so
10. After the first smoking is done, take an aluminum foil and wrap up the meat forming a watertight seal
11. Place the meat in the middle of your foil and bring the edges to the top, cupping up the meat complete
12. Pour 1 cup of sauce over the beef and tight it up
13. Place the package back into your smoker and smoke for 2 hours until the meat quickly pulls off from the bone
14. Once done, remove it from the smoker and pull off the pork, discarding the bone and fat
15. Place the meat chunks in a pan and pour 1 cup of sauce for every 4 pound of meat
16. Heat until simmering and serve immediately!

Nutrition: Calories: 1098 Fats: 86g Carbs: 38g Fiber: 3g

GRILL LAMB RECIPES

Seven Spice Grilled Lamb Chops with Parsley Salad

Preparation Time: 3 hours
Cooking Time: 1 hour
Servings: 6

Ingredients

- 1 cup plain whole-milk yogurt (not Greek)
- 1 tsp. grounded black pepper
- 1 tsp. ground coriander
- 1 tsp. ground cumin
- 1 tsp. paprika
- ½ tsp. ground cardamom
- ½ tsp. ground cinnamon
- ½ tsp. ground nutmeg
- 12 untrimmed lamb rib chops (about three lb.), patted dry
- Kosher salt
- One thinly sliced small red onion
- 1 cup coarsely chopped parsley
- 1 tbsp. of fresh lemon juice
- 2 tsp. sumac

Directions:

1. Mix the yogurt, grounded black pepper, coriander, cumin, paprika, cardamom, cinnamon, and nutmeg in a big bowl.
2. Season the two facets of lamb chops with salt and add them to the bowl with marinade. Turn lamb in marinade, cowl, and kick back for at least 3 hours and no greater than 12 hours.
3. Let the lamb sit down at room temperature for one hour earlier than grilling.
4. Set up the grill for medium-high warmness. Grill the lamb, around three minutes for each aspect, and let it rest for five or 10 minutes.
5. In the meantime, blend the onion, parsley, lemon juice, and sumac with a touch of salt in a medium bowl. Serve the lamb chops with parsley salad on top.

Nutrition: Energy (calories): 284 kcal Protein: 36.49 g Fat: 12.84 g Carbohydrates: 3.76 g

Smoked Loin Lamb Chops

Preparation Time: 20 Minutes
Cooking Time: 1 Hour & 20 Minutes
Servings: 6 Persons

Ingredients

- 10 to 12 Lamb loin chops
- Jeff's Original rub recipe
- Rosemary, finely chopped
- Olive oil
- Coarse kosher salt

Directions

1. Place the chops on a cookie sheet or cooling rack.
2. To dry brine, generously sprinkle the pinnacle of chops with salt.
3. Place in a refrigerator for an hour or two.
4. Once done, put off the coated meat from the fridge; ensure that you don't rinse the meat.
5. Prepare an infusion of olive oil and rosemary by pouring about ¼ cup of the olive oil on the pinnacle of 1 tablespoon of the chopped rosemary; set the combination apart and let sit for an hour.
6. Brush the organized aggregate on pinnacle & facets of your lamb chops.
7. Generously sprinkle the pinnacle, aspects, and bottom of chops with the rub.
8. Preheat your smoker at 225 F on oblique heat.
9. For outstanding results, ensure which you use a combination of apple and pecan for the smoke.
10. Cook the lined chops for forty to 50 minutes until the chops' internal temperature displays 138 F.
11. Let relaxation on the counter for 5 to 7 minutes, with foil tented.
12. Serve warm and enjoy.

Nutrition: 652 Calories 53g Total Fat 693mg Potassium 0.2g Total Carbohydrates 41g Protein

GRILL POULTRY RECIPES

Wood Pellet Grilled Buffalo Chicken Leg

Preparation Time: 5 minutesCooking Time: 25 minutes Servings: 6

Ingredients:

- 12 chicken legs
- 1/2 tbsp salt
- 1 tbsp buffalo seasoning
- 1 cup buffalo sauce

Directions:

1. Preheat your wood pellet grill to 325°F.
2. Toss the legs in salt and buffalo seasoning then place them on the preheated grill.
3. Grill for 40 minutes ensuring you turn them twice through the cooking.
4. Brush the legs with buffalo sauce and cook for an additional 10 minutes or until the internal temperature reaches 165°F.
5. Remove the legs from the grill, brush with more sauce, and serve when hot.

Nutrition: Calories: 956 Cal Fat: 47 g Carbohydrates: 1 g Protein: 124 g Fiber: 0 g

Wood Pellet Chile Lime Chicken

Preparation Time: 2 minutes
Cooking Time: 15 minutes
Servings: 1
Ingredients:

- 1 chicken breast
- 1 tbsp oil
- 1 tbsp chile-lime seasoning

Directions:

1. Preheat your wood pellet to 400°F.
2. Brush the chicken breast with oil on all sides.
3. Sprinkle with seasoning and salt to taste.
4. Grill for 7 minutes per side or until the internal temperature reaches 165°F.
5. Serve when hot or cold and enjoy.

Nutrition: Calories: 131 Cal Fat: 5 g Carbohydrates: 4 g Protein: 19 g Fiber: 1 g

Wood Pellet Sheet Pan Chicken Fajitas

Preparation Time: 10 minutes
Cooking Time: 10 minutes
Servings: 10

Ingredients:

- 2 tbsp oil
- 2 tbsp chile margarita seasoning
- 1 tbsp salt
- 1/2 tbsp onion powder
- 1/2 tbsp garlic, granulated
- 2-pound chicken breast, thinly sliced
- 1 red bell pepper, seeded and sliced
- 1 orange bell pepper
- 1 onion, sliced

Directions:

1. Preheat the wood pellet to 450°F.
2. Meanwhile, mix oil and seasoning then toss the chicken and the peppers.
3. Line a sheet pan with foil then place it in the preheated grill. Let it heat for 10 minutes with the grill's lid closed.
4. Open the grill and place the chicken with the veggies on the pan in a single layer.
5. Cook for 10 minutes or until the chicken is cooked and no longer pink.
6. Remove from grill and serve with tortilla or your favorite fixings.

Nutrition: Calories: 211 Cal Fat: 6 g Carbohydrates: 5 g Protein: 29 g Fiber: 1 g

Buffalo Chicken Flatbread

Preparation Time: 5 minutes
Cooking Time: 30 minutes
Servings: 6
Ingredients:

- 6 mini pita bread
- 1-1/2 cups buffalo sauce
- 4 cups chicken breasts, cooked and cubed
- 3 cups mozzarella cheese
- Blue cheese for drizzling

Directions:

1. Preheat the wood pellet grill to 375-400°F.
2. Place the breads on a flat surface and evenly spread sauce over all of them.
3. Toss the chicken with the remaining buffalo sauce and place it on the pita breads.
4. Top with cheese then place the breads on the grill but indirectly from the heat. Close the grill lid.
5. Cook for 7 minutes or until the cheese has melted and the edges are toasty.
6. Remove from grill and drizzle with blue cheese. Serve and enjoy.

Nutrition: Calories: 254 Cal Fat: 13 g Carbohydrates: 4 g Protein: 33 g Fiber: 3 g

Wood Pellet Grilled Buffalo Chicken

Preparation Time: 5
minutesCooking Time:
20 minutes Servings: 6
Ingredients:

- 5 chicken breasts, boneless and skinless
- 2 tbsp homemade barbeque rub
- 1 cup homemade Cholula buffalo sauce

Directions:

1. Preheat the wood pellet grill to 400°F.
2. Slice the chicken into long strips and season with barbeque rub.
3. Place the chicken on the grill and paint both sides with buffalo sauce.
4. Cook for 4 minutes with the grill closed. Cook while flipping and painting with buffalo sauce every 5 minutes until the internal temperature reaches 165°F.
5. Remove from the grill and serve when warm. Enjoy.

Nutrition: Calories: 176 Cal Fat: 4 g Carbohydrates: 1 g Protein: 32 g Fiber: 0 g

Beer Can Chicken

Preparation Time: 10 minutes
Cooking Time: 1 hour and 15 minutes
Servings: 6
Ingredients:

- 5-pound chicken
- 1/2 cup dry chicken rub
- 1 can beer

Directions:

1. Preheat your wood pellet grill on smoke for 5 minutes with the lid open.
2. The lid must then be closed and then preheated up to 450 degrees Fahrenheit
3. Pour out half of the beer then shove the can in the chicken and use the legs like a tripod.
4. Place the chicken on the grill until the internal temperature reaches 165°F.
5. Remove from the grill and let rest for 20 minutes before serving. Enjoy.

Nutrition: Calories: 882 Cal Fat: 51 g Carbohydrates: 2 g Protein: 94 g Fiber: 0 g

Wood Pellet Chicken Wings with Spicy Miso

Preparation Time: 15 minutesCooking Time: 25 minutes Servings:6

Ingredients:

- 2-pound chicken wings
- 3/4 cup soy
- 1/2 cup pineapple juice
- 1 tbsp sriracha
- 1/8 cup miso
- 1/8 cup gochujang
- 1/2 cup water
- 1/2 cup oil
- Togarashi

Directions:

1. Mix all ingredients then toss the chicken wings until well coated. Refrigerate for 12 minutes.
2. Preheat your wood pellet grill to 375°F.
3. Place the chicken wings on the grill grates and close the lid. Cook until the internal temperature reaches 165°F.
4. Remove the wings from the grill and sprinkle with togarashi.
5. Serve when hot and enjoy.

Nutrition: Calories: 704 Cal Fat: 56 g Carbohydrates: 24 g Protein: 27 g Fiber: 1 g

Bacon-wrapped Chicken Tenders

Preparation Time: 25 minutes
Cooking Time: 30 minutes
Servings: 6
Ingredients:

- 1-pound chicken tenders
- 10 strips bacon
- 1/2 tbsp Italian seasoning
- 1/2 tbsp black pepper
- 1/2 tbsp salt
- 1 tbsp paprika
- 1 tbsp onion powder
- 1 tbsp garlic powder
- 1/3 cup light brown sugar
- 1 tbsp chili powder

Directions:

1. Preheat your wood pellet smoker to 350°F.
2. Mix seasonings
3. Sprinkle the mixture on all sides of chicken tenders
4. Wrap each chicken tender with a strip of bacon
5. Place them on the smoker and smoker for 30 minutes with the lid closed or until the chicken is cooked.
6. Serve and enjoy.

Nutrition: Calories: 206 Cal Fat: 7.9 g Carbohydrates: 1.5 g Protein: 30.3 g Fiber: 0 g

TURKEY, RABBIT AND VEAL

Tailgate Smoked Young Turkey

Preparation Time: 20 Minutes

Cooking Time: 4 To 4 Hours 30 Minutes

Servings: 6

Ingredients:

- 1 fresh or thawed frozen young turkey
- 6 glasses of extra virgin olive oil with roasted garlic flavor
- 6 original Yang dry lab or poultry seasonings

Directions:

1. Remove excess fat and skin from turkey breasts and cavities.
2. Slowly separate the skin of the turkey to its breast and a quarter of the leg, leaving the skin intact.
3. Apply olive oil to the chest, under the skin and on the skin.
4. Gently rub or season to the chest cavity, under the skin and on the skin.
5. Set up tailgate Blackstone smoker grill for indirect cooking and smoking. Preheat to 225 ° F using apple or cherry Blackstones.
6. Put the turkey meat on the grill with the chest up.
7. Suck the turkey for 4-4 hours at 225 ° F until the thickest part of the turkey's chest reaches an internal temperature of 170 ° F and the juice is clear.
8. Before engraving, place the turkey under a loose foil tent for 20 minutes

Nutrition: Calories: 240 Carbs: 27g Fat: 9g Protein: 15g

Roast Turkey Orange

Preparation Time: 30 Minutes
Cooking Time: 2 hours 30 minutes
Servings:
Ingredients:

- 1 Frozen Long Island turkey
- 3 tablespoons west
- 1 large orange, cut into wedges
- Three celery stems chopped into large chunks
- Half a small red onion, a quarter
- Orange sauce:
- 2 orange cups
- 2 tablespoons soy sauce
- 2 tablespoons orange marmalade
- 2 tablespoons honey
- 3 teaspoons grated raw

Directions:

1. Remove the nibble from the turkey's cavity and neck and retain or discard for another use. Wash the duck and pat some dry paper towel.
2. Remove excess fat from tail, neck and cavity. Use a sharp scalpel knife tip to pierce the turkey's skin entirely, so that it does not penetrate the duck's meat, to help dissolve the fat layer beneath the skin.
3. Add the seasoning inside the cavity with one cup of rub or seasoning.
4. Season the outside of the turkey with the remaining friction or seasoning.
5. Fill the cavity with orange wedges, celery and onion. Duck legs are tied with butcher twine to make filling easier. Place the turkey's breast up on a small rack of shallow roast bread.
6. To make the sauce, mix the ingredients in the saucepan over low heat and cook until the sauce is thick and syrupy. Set aside and let cool.
7. Set the Blackstone smoker grill for indirect cooking and use the Blackstones to preheat to 350
   ° F.
8. Roast the turkey at 350 ° F for 2 hours.
9. After 2 hours, brush the turkey freely with orange sauce.
10. Roast the orange glass turkey for another 30 minutes, making sure that the inside temperature of the thickest part of the leg reaches 165 ° F.
11. Place turkey under loose foil tent for 20 minutes before serving.
12. Discard the orange wedge, celery and onion. Serve with a quarter of turkey with poultry scissors.

Nutrition: Calories: 216 Carbs: 2g Fat: 11g Protein: 34g

Smoked Whole Chicken with Honey Glaze

Preparation Time: 30 minutes
Cooking Time: 3 Hours
Servings: 1

Ingredients:

- 1 4 pounds of chicken with the giblets thoroughly removed and patted dry
- 1 ½ lemon
- 1 tablespoon of honey
- 4 tablespoons of unsalted butter
- 4 tablespoon of chicken seasoning

Directions:

1. Fire up your smoker and set the temperature to 225 degrees F
2. Take a small saucepan and melt the butter along with honey over a low flame
3. Now squeeze ½ lemon in this mixture and then move it from the heat source
4. Take the chicken and smoke by keeping the skin side down. Do so until the chicken turns light brown and the skin starts to release from the grate.
5. Turn the chicken over and apply the honey butter mixture to it
6. Continue to smoke it making sure to taste it every 45 minutes until the thickest core reaches a temperature of 160 degrees F
7. Now remove the chicken from the grill and let it rest for 5 minutes
8. Serve with the leftover sliced lemon and enjoy

Nutrition: Carbohydrates: 29 g Protein: 19 g Sodium: 25 mg Cholesterol: 19 mg

Slow Roasted Shawarma

Preparation Time: 30 minutes
Cooking Time: 4 Hours
Servings: 1
Ingredients:

- 5 ½ lbs. of chicken thighs; boneless, skinless
- 4 ½ lbs. of lamb fat
- Pita bread
- 5 ½ lbs. of top sirloin
- 2 yellow onions; large
- 4 tablespoons of rub
- Desired toppings like pickles, tomatoes, fries, salad and more

Directions:

1. Slice the meat and fat into ½" slices and place then in 3 separate bowls
2. Season each of the bowls with the rub and massage the rub into the meat to make sure it seeps well
3. Now place half of the onion at the base of each half skewer. This will make for a firm base
4. Add 2 layers from each of the bowls at a time
5. Make the track as symmetrical as you can
6. Now, put the other 2 half onions at the top of this
7. Wrap it in a plastic wrap and let it refrigerate overnight
8. Set the grill to preheat keeping the temperature to 275 degrees F
9. Lay the shawarma on the grill grate and let it cook for approx. 4 hours. Make sure to turn it at least once
10. Remove from the grill and shoot the temperature to 445 degrees F
11. Now place a cast iron griddle on the grill grate and pour it with olive oil
12. When the griddle has turned hot, place the whole shawarma on the cast iron and smoke it for 5 to 10 minutes per side
13. Remove from the grill and slice off the edges
14. Repeat the same with the leftover shawarma
15. Serve in pita bread and add the chosen toppings
16. Enjoy

Nutrition: Carbohydrates: 39 g Protein: 29 g Sodium: 15 mg Cholesterol: 19 mg

Duck Poppers

Preparation Time: 30 minutes
Cooking Time: 4 Hours
Servings: 1
Ingredients:

- 8 – 10 pieces of bacon, cut event into same-sized pieces measuring 4 inches each
- 3 duck breasts; boneless and with skin removed and sliced into strips measuring ½ inches
- Sriracha sauce
- 6 de-seeded jalapenos, with the top cut off and sliced into strips

Directions:

1. Wrap the bacon around one trip of pepper and one slice of duck
2. Secure it firmly with the help of a toothpick
3. Fire the grill on low flame and keep this wrap and grill it for half an hour until the bacon turns crisp
4. Rotate often to ensure even cooking
5. Serve with sriracha sauce

Nutrition: Carbohydrates: 39 g Protein: 29 g Sodium: 15 mg Cholesterol: 19 mg

Baked Garlic Parmesan Wings

Preparation Time: 30 minutes
Cooking Time: 3 Hours
Servings: 1
Ingredients:

- For the chicken wings
- 5lbs. of chicken wings
- ½ cup of chicken rub
- For the garnish
- 1 cup of shredded parmesan cheese
- 3 tablespoons of chopped parsley
- For the sauce
- 10 cloves of finely diced garlic
- 1 cup of butter
- 2 tablespoon of chicken rub

Directions:

1. Set the grill on preheat by keeping the temperature to high
2. Take a large bowl and toss the wings in it along with the chicken rub
3. Now place the wings directly on the grill grate and cook it for 10 minutes
4. Flip it and cook for the ten minutes
5. Check the internal temperature and it needs to reach in the range of 165 to 180 degrees F
6. For the garlic sauce
7. Take a midsized saucepan and mix garlic, butter, and the leftover rub.
8. Cook it over medium heat on a stovetop
9. Cook for 10 minutes while stirring in between to avoid the making of lumps
10. Now when the wings have been cooked, remove them from the grill and place in a large bowl
11. Toss the wings with garlic sauce along with parsley and parmesan cheese
12. Serve and enjoy

Nutrition: Carbohydrates: 19 g Protein: 29 g Sodium: 15 mg Cholesterol: 59 mg

Grilled Chicken in Blackstone

Preparation Time: 10 minutes
Cooking Time: 30 minutes
Servings: 8
Ingredients:

- Whole chicken - 4-5 lbs.
- Grilled chicken mix

Directions:

1. Preheat the Blackstone grill with the 'smoke' option for 5 minutes.
2. Preheat another 10 minutes and keep the temperature on high until it reaches 450 degrees.
3. Use baker's twine to tie the chicken's legs together.
4. Keep the breast side up when you place the chicken in the grill.
5. Grill for 70 minutes. Do not open the grill during this process.
6. Check the temperature of your grilled chicken. Make sure it is 165 degrees. If not, leave the chicken in for longer.
7. Carefully take the chicken out of the grill.
8. Set aside for 15 minutes.
9. Cut and serve.

Nutrition: Carbohydrates: 0 g Protein: 107 g Fat: 0 g Sodium: 320 mg Cholesterol: 346 mg

Chicken Wings in Blackstone

Preparation Time: 10 minutes
Cooking Time: 50 minutes
Servings: 1
Ingredients:

- Chicken wings - 6-8 lbs.
- Canola oil – 1/3 cup
- Barbeque seasoning mix - 1 tablespoon

Directions:

1. Combine the seasonings and oil in one large bowl.
2. Put the chicken wings in the bowl and mix well.
3. Turn your Blackstone to the 'smoke' setting and leave it on for 4-5 minutes.
4. Set the heat to 350 degrees and leave it to preheat for 15 minutes with the lid closed.
5. Place the wings on the grill with enough space between the pieces.
6. Let it cook for 45 minutes or until the skin looks crispy.
7. Remove from the grill and serve with your choice of sides.

Nutrition: Protein: 33 g Fat: 8 g Sodium: 134 mg Cholesterol: 141 mg

SMOKING   RECIPES

Fire and Ice Smoked Salmon

Preparation Time: 6 hours
Cooking Time: 50 minutes
Servings: 7
Ingredients:

- ½ a cup of brown sugar
- 2 tablespoons of salt
- 2 tablespoon of crushed red pepper flakes
- Mint leaves
- ¼ cup of brandy
- 1 (4 pounds) salmon side with bones removed
- 2 cups of alder wood chips, soaked up in water

Directions:

1. Take a medium bowl and mix in the brown sugar, crushed red pepper flakes, salt, mint leaves and brandy until a paste form. Coat the paste on all sides of the salmon and wrap the Salmon up in plastic wrap.
2. Let it refrigerate for at least 4 hours or overnight. Preheat your smoker to high heat and oil up the grate. Adsoaked alder chips to your heat box and wait until smoke starts to appear.
3. Turn the heat to your lowest setting and place the salmon on the grate. Lock up the lid and let your Salmon smoke for about 45 minutes.

Nutrition: Calories: 370 Cal Fat: 28 g Carbohydrates: 1 g Protein: 23 g Fiber: 0 g

Bradley Maple Cure Smoked Salmon

Preparation Time: 2 hours

Cooking Time: 1 hour and 30 minutes

Servings: 6

Ingredients:

- 1 large sized salmon fillet
- 1 quart of water
- ½ a cup of pickling and canning salt
- ½ a cup of maple syrup
- ¼ cup of dark rum
- ¼ cup of lemon juice
- 10 whole cloves
- 10 whole allspice berries
- 1 bay leaf

Directions:

1. Take a medium sized bowl and add the brine ingredients. Mix them well. Place the salmon fillet in a cover with brine.
2. Cover it up and let it refrigerate for about 2 hours. Remove the Salmon and pat dry then air dry for 1 hour.
3. Preheat your smoker to a temperature of 180 degrees Fahrenheit and add Bradley Maple-Flavored briquettes. Smoke the salmon for about 1 and a ½ hour.

Nutrition: Calories: 223 Cal Fat: 7 g Carbohydrates: 15 g Protein: 21 g Fiber: 0 g

Smoked Teriyaki Tuna

Preparation Time: 5-7 hours
Cooking Time: 2 hours
Servings: 4
Ingredients:

- Tuna steaks, 1 oz.
- 2 c. marinade, teriyaki
- Alder wood chips soaked in water

Directions:

1. Slice tuna into thick slices of 2 inch. Place your tuna slices and marinade then set in your fridge for about 3 hours
2. After 3 hours, remove the tuna from the marinade and pat dry. Let the tuna air dry in your fridge for 2-4 hours. Preheat your smoker to 180 degrees Fahrenheit
3. Place the Tuna on a Teflon-coated fiberglass and place them directly on your grill grates. Smoke the Tuna for about an hour until the internal temperature reaches 145 degrees Fahrenheit.
4. Remove the tuna from your grill and let them rest for 10 minutes. Serve!

Nutrition: Calories: 249 Cal Fat: 3 g Carbohydrates: 33 g Protein: 21 g Fiber: 0 g

Cold Hot Smoked Salmon

Preparation Time: 16 hoursCooking Time: 8 hours Servings: 4

Ingredients:

- 5 pound of fresh sockeye (red) salmon fillets
- For trout Brine
- 4 cups of filtered water
- 1 cup of soy sauce
- ½ a cup of pickling kosher salt
- ½ a cup of brown sugar
- 2 tablespoon of garlic powder
- 2 tablespoon of onion powder
- 1 teaspoon of cayenne pepper

Directions:

1. Combine all of the ingredients listed under trout brine in two different 1-gallon bags. Store it in your fridge. Cut up the Salmon fillets into 3-4-inch pieces. Place your salmon pieces into your 1-gallon container of trout brine and let it keep in your fridge for 8 hours.
2. Rotate the Salmon and pat them dry using a kitchen towel for 8 hours
3. Configure your pellet smoker for indirect cooking. Remove your salmon pieces of from your fridge Preheat your smoker to a temperature of 180 degrees Fahrenheit
4. Once a cold smoke at 70 degrees Fahrenheit starts smoke your fillets
5. Keep smoking it until the internal temperature reaches 145 degrees Fahrenheit.
6. Remove the Salmon from your smoker and let it rest for 10 minutes

Nutrition: Calories: 849 Cal Fat: 45 g Carbohydrates: 51 g Protein: 46 g Fiber: 0 g

Smoked Up Salmon and Dungeness Crab Chowder

Preparation Time: 30 minutes
Cooking Time: 45 minutes
Servings: 6
Ingredients:

- 4 gallons of water
- 3 fresh Dungeness crabs
- 1 cup of rock salt
- 3 cups of Cold-Hot Smoked Salmon
- 3 cups of ocean clam juice
- 5 diced celery stalks
- 1 yellow diced onion
- 2 peeled and diced large sized russet potatoes
- 14 ounces of sweet corn
- 12 ounce of clam chowder dry soup mix
- 4 bacon slices crumbled and cooked

Directions:

1. Bring 4 gallons of water and rock salt to a boil. Add the Dungeness crab and boil for 20 minutes
2. Remove the crabs , let it cool and clean the crabs and pick out crab meat. Place it over high heat.
3. Add clam juice, 5 cups of water, diced potatoes, diced celery, and onion. Bring the mix to a boil as well. Add corn to the liquid and boil.
4. Whisk in the clam chowder and keep mixing everything. Simmer on low for about 15 minutes and add the crumbled bacon. Add bacon, garnish with ½ cup flaked smoked salmon and ½ cup Dungeness crabmeat. Serve!

Nutrition: Calories: 174 Cal Fat: 5 g Carbohydrates: 12 g Protein: 8 g Fiber: 0 g

Alder Wood Smoked Bony Trout

Preparation Time: 4 hours **Cooking Time: 2 hours** **Servings: 4**

Ingredients:

- 4 fresh boned whole trout with their skin on
- For trout Brine
- 4 cups of filtered water
- 1 cup of soy sauce
- ½ a cup of pickling kosher salt
- ½ a cup of brown sugar
- 2 tablespoon of garlic powder
- 2 tablespoon of onion powder
- 1 teaspoon of cayenne pepper

Directions:

1. Combine all of the ingredients listed under trout brine in two different 1-gallon bags.
2. Store it in your fridge.
3. Place your trout in the sealable bag with trout brine and place the bag in a shallow dish.
4. Let it refrigerate for about 2 hours, making sure to rotate it after 30 minutes.
5. Remove them from your brine and pat them dry using kitchen towels.
6. Air Dry your brine trout in your fridge uncovered for about 2 hours.
7. Preheat your smoker to a temperature of 180 degrees Fahrenheit using alder pellets.
8. The pit temperature of should be 180 degrees Fahrenheit and the cold smoke should be 70 degrees Fahrenheit.
9. Cold smoke your prepared trout for 90 minutes.
10. After 90 minutes transfer the cold smoked boned trout pellets to your smoker grill are and increase the smoker temperature to 225 degrees Fahrenheit.
11. Keep cooking until the internal temperature reaches 145 degrees Fahrenheit in the thickest parts.
12. Remove the trout from the grill and let them rest for 5 minutes.
13. Serve!

Nutrition: Calories: 508 Cal Fat: 23 g Carbohydrates: 47 g Protein: 15 g Fiber: 0 g

FISH AND SEAFOOD RECIPES

Garlic Salmon

Preparation Time: 10 minutes
Cooking Time: 55 minutes
Servings: 4

Ingredients:

- 3 pounds salmon fillets, skin on
- 2 tbsp. minced garlic
- 1/2 tablespoons minced parsley
- 4 tbsp. seafood seasoning
- 1/4 cup olive oil

Directions:

1. Open the smoker's hopper, add dry pallets, make sure ash-can is in place, open the ash damper, power on the smoker, and close the ash damper.
2. Set the temperature of the smoker to 450 degrees F, switch smoker to open flame cooking mode, press the open flame 3, remove the grill grates and the batch, replace batch with direct flame insert, then return grates on the grill in the lower position and let preheat for 30 minutes or until the green light on the dial blinks that indicate smoker has reached to set temperature.
3. Meanwhile, take a baking sheet, line it with a parchment sheet and place salmon on it, skin-side down, and then season salmon with seafood seasoning on both sides.
4. Stir together garlic, parsley, and oil until combined, and then brush this mixture on the salmon fillets.
5. Place baking sheet containing salmon fillets on the smoker grill, shut with lid, and smoke for 25 minutes or until the salmon's internal temperature reaches 140 degrees F.
6. When done, transfer salmon fillets to a dish, brush with more garlic-oil mixture and serve with lemon wedges.

Nutrition: Calories: 130, Saturated Fat: 1 g; Protein: 13 g; Carbs: 6 g; Fiber: 0 g; Sugar: 2 g

Vodka Brined Salmon

Preparation Time: 4 hours 10 minutes
Cooking Time: 2 hours
Servings: 6

Ingredients:

- 2 pounds salmon fillets
- 1/2 cup salt
- 1 cup brown sugar
- 1 tbsp. ground black pepper
- 1 cup vodka

Directions:

1. Pour vodka into a bowl, add salt, sugar, and black pepper and stir until mixed.
2. Place salmon in a large plastic bag, pour in vodka mixture, then seal the bag, turn it upside down to coat salmon with vodka mixture and let marinate in the refrigerator for 4 hours.
3. When ready to cook, open the smoker's hopper, add dry pallets, make sure the ash-can is in place, open the ash damper, power on the smoker, and close the ash damper.
4. Set the smoker's temperature to 180 degrees F, let preheat for 30 minutes or until the green light on the dial blinks that indicate the smoker has reached to set temperature.
5. Remove salmon from the marinade, place it on the smoker grill, and smoke for 30 minutes.
6. Then, increase the smoker's temperature to 225 degrees F and continue smoking the salmon for 1 hour or until the salmon's internal temperature reaches 140 degrees F.
7. When done, transfer salmon to a dish and serve with lemon wedges.

Nutrition: Calories: 456.3; Total Fat: 11.2 g; Saturated Fat: 2 g; Protein: 33.1 g; Carbs: 35.4 g; Fiber: 0 g; Sugar: 35.5 g

Smoked Trout

Preparation Time: 10 minutes
Cooking Time: 2 hours 30 minutes
Servings: 4-6

Ingredients:

- Four trout filets, skin on one side
- ½ teaspoon onion powder
- 1 ½ teaspoon salt
- ½ teaspoon red chili powder
- 2 tbsp. brown sugar
- 1 tsp. dried oregano
- ¼ teaspoon ground black pepper
- ½ teaspoon dried thyme

Directions:

1. Open the smoker's hopper, add dry pallets, make sure ash-can is in place, open the ash damper, power on the smoker, and close the ash damper.
2. Set the smoker's temperature to 225 degrees F, let preheat for 30 minutes or until the green light on the dial blinks that indicate the smoker has reached to set temperature.
3. Meanwhile, prepare the trout and for this, remove any pin bones by using a noose plier.
4. Stir together the remaining ingredients until mixed and then rub into the top surface.
5. Place trout fillets on the smoker grill, shut with lid, and smoke for 2 hours or until the trout's internal temperature reaches 140 degrees F.
6. When done, transfer trout to a dish and serve with lemon wedges.

Nutrition: Calories: 196; Total Fat: 4.8 g; Saturated Fat: 1.2 g; Protein: 35.2 g; Carbs: 0 g; Fiber: 0 g; Sugar: 3 g

Sesame Crusted Halibut

Preparation Time: 10 minutes
Cooking Time: 2 hours 30 minutes
Servings: 4

Ingredients:

For the Halibut:

- 1 ½ pound halibut fillet, cut into equal four pieces
- ½ cup pickled ginger
- ½ teaspoon salt
- ½ cup toasted sesame seeds
- 1 tbsp. olive oil
- 1 tsp. sesame oil

For the Mayo Dip:

- 1 tbsp. soy sauce
- ¼ cup tahini paste
- 2 tbsp. lemon juice
- 1 ½ cup olive oil
- Two egg yolks

Directions:

1. Open the smoker's hopper, add dry pallets, make sure ash-can is in place, open the ash damper, power on the smoker, and close the ash damper.
2. Set the temperature of the smoker to 225 degrees F, switch smoker to open flame cooking mode, press the open flame 3, remove the grill grates and the batch, replace batch with direct flame insert, then return grates on the grill in the lower position and let preheat for 30 minutes or until the green light on the dial blinks that indicate smoker has reached to set temperature.
3. Meanwhile, place sesame seeds in a mortar; add salt and crush with a pestle until just ground, not powder.
4. Stir together sesame oil and olive oil, then brush the mixture on all sides of fillets and sprinkle with sesame seeds until well coated.
5. Place prepared halibut fillets on the smoker grill, shut with lid, and smoke for 2 hours and 30 minutes, or until the fish's internal temperature reaches 145 degrees F.
6. Meanwhile, prepare the mayonnaise dip and for this, place all its ingredients in a food processor except for oil and blend until smooth.
7. Then gradually blend in oil until incorporated and thick and creamy mixture comes together, and then tip the sauce in a bowl.
8. When done, transfer halibut to a dish and serve with pickled ginger and prepared mayonnaise dip.

Nutrition: Calories: 284.6; Total Fat: 15.6 g; Saturated Fat: 2.2 g; Protein: 29.6 g; Carbs: 4.2 g; Fiber: 1 g; Sugar: 0.5 g

Smoked Lobster Roll

Preparation Time: 10 minutes
Cooking Time: 1 hour 30 minutes
Servings: 4

Ingredients:

- Three lobster tails, each about 8 ounces
- ½ tablespoon minced garlic
- 1/2 cup butter, unsalted, melted
- 1 cup mayonnaise
- One green onion, chopped
- 1 tsp. dill
- 1/2 lemon, juiced
- 1 ½ teaspoon salt
- ¾ teaspoon ground black pepper
- Four buns halved, toasted

Directions:

1. Open the smoker's hopper, add dry pallets, make sure ash-can is in place, and then open the ash damper, power on the smoker, and close the ash damper.
2. Set the temperature of the smoker to 450 degrees F, switch smoker to open flame cooking mode, press the open flame 3, remove the grill grates and the batch, replace batch with direct flame insert, then return grates on the grill in the lower position and let preheat for 30 minutes or until the green light on the dial blinks that indicate smoker has reached to set temperature.
3. Meanwhile, prepare the lobster tails and for this, use a sharp knife to expose the meat by splitting the bottom.
4. Stir together butter and garlic, brush this mixture generously on the meat in the tail, and place it on the smoker grill.
5. Shut the smoker with a lid and smoke for 1 hour or until the crab's internal temperature reaches 135 degrees F.
6. When done, transfer lobster tails to a dish, then cool completely and transfer its meat to a bowl.
7. Add onion, salt, black pepper, dill, lemon juice, and mayonnaise and stir until mixed.
8. Serve the lobster meat in buns.

Nutrition: Calories: 378.7; Total Fat: 18.1 g; Saturated Fat: 2 g; Protein: 10.3 g; Carbs: 42.7 g; Fiber: 1.3 g; Sugar: 11 g

Lobster Tail

Preparation Time: 10 minutes
Cooking Time: 1 hour and 5 minutes
Servings: 2

Ingredients:

- Two lobster tails, each about 8-ounce
- 1/4 teaspoon old bay seasoning
- 1/4 teaspoon garlic salt
- 1/4 teaspoon ground black pepper
- 8 tbsp. butter, unsalted
- 1 tsp. paprika
- 2 tbsp. lemon juice
- 2 tbsp. chopped parsley

Directions:

1. Open the smoker's hopper, add dry pallets, make sure ash-can is in place, and then open the ash damper, power on the smoker, and close the ash damper.
2. Set the temperature of the smoker to 450 degrees F, switch smoker to open flame cooking mode, press the open flame 3, remove the grill grates and the batch, replace batch with direct flame insert, then return grates on the grill in the lower position and let preheat for 30 minutes or until the green light on the dial blinks that indicate smoker has reached to set temperature.
3. Meanwhile, prepare the lobster and for this, use kitchen shears to cut down the middle of the shell and then lift out the meat by using your fingers from it but keep it attached at the base of the tail.
4. Then butterfly the crab meat by making a slit down the middle and place the lobster tails on a baking sheet.
5. Put a saucepan over medium-low heat, add butter and when it melts, add garlic salt, black pepper, paprika, parsley, old bay seasoning, and lemon juice, stir well and remove the pan from the heat.
6. Spoon 1 tablespoon of the butter sauce over each lobster tail, then transfer lobster tails to the smoker grill from the baking sheet and shut with lid.
7. Smoke the lobster tails for 30 minutes or until its meat is white.
8. When done, transfer lobster tails to a dish and serve with remaining butter sauce.

Nutrition: Calories: 131.9; Total Fat: 4 g; Saturated Fat: 1 g; Protein: 20.1 g; Carbs: 1.4 g; Fiber: 0.1 g; Sugar: 0 g

Cajun Smoked Shrimps

Preparation Time: 4 hours 15 minutes
Cooking Time: 53 minutes
Servings: 4

Ingredients:

- 2 pounds shrimp, peeled, deveined

For the Marinade:

- 1 tsp. minced garlic
- 1 tsp. salt
- 1 tbsp. Cajun shake
- One lemon, juiced
- 4 tbsp. olive oil

Directions:

1. Place and combine all the ingredients for the marinade in a small bowl and stir until mixed.
2. Place the shrimps in a large plastic bag, pour in marinade, seal the bag, then turn it upside down to coat the shrimps and let marinate for 4 hours in the refrigerator.
3. When ready to cook, open the smoker's hopper, add dry pallets, make sure the ash-can is in place, open the ash damper, power on the smoker, and close the ash damper.
4. Set the temperature of the smoker to 450 degrees F, switch smoker to open flame cooking mode, press the open flame 3, remove the grill grates and the batch, replace batch with direct flame insert, then return grates on the grill in the lower position and let preheat for 30 minutes or until the green light on the dial blinks that indicate smoker has reached to set temperature.
5. Remove shrimps from the marinade, place them on the smoker grill, shut with lid, and smoke for 15 minutes.
6. When done, transfer shrimps to a dish, let cool for 5 minutes, and thread the shrimps on skewers.
7. Place shrimp skewers on the grill grate and smoke for 4 minutes per side or until shrimps are opaque.
8. Serve straight away.

Nutrition: Calories: 92; Total Fat: 7.6 g; Saturated Fat: 1.1 g; Protein: 4.6 g; Carbs: 2.2 g; Fiber: 0.8 g; Sugar: 0.3 g

Mango Chipotle Shrimp Skewers

Preparation Time: 4 hours 10 minutes
Cooking Time: 1 hour
Servings: 6

Ingredients:

- 1-pound shrimp, peeled, deveined
- 3 tbsp. minced garlic
- 1 tbsp. mango chipotle rub
- ¾ teaspoon salt
- ½ cup butter, unsalted

Directions:

1. Place butter in a heatproof bowl, microwave for 1 minute or more until it melts, and then adds garlic, salt, and chipotle rub and stir until combined.
2. Place shrimps in a large plastic bag, add butter mixture, seal the bag, then turn it upside down to coat the shrimps and let marinate for 4 hours in the refrigerator.
3. When ready to cook, open the smoker's hopper, add dry pallets, make sure the ash-can is in place, open the ash damper, power on the smoker, and close the ash damper.
4. Set the smoker's temperature to 375 degrees F, let preheat for 30 minutes, then set it to 225 degrees F and continue preheating for 20 minutes or until the green light on the dial blinks that indicate the smoker has reached to set temperature.
5. Remove shrimps from the marinade, thread them onto soaked wooden skewers and place them on the smoker grill.
6. Shut the smoker with a lid and smoke for 20 to 30 minutes or until shrimps are slightly pink.
7. Serve straight away.

Nutrition: Calories: 157.2; Total Fat: 3.8 g; Saturated Fat: 0.6 g; Protein: 24.2 g; Carbs: 5.1 g; Fiber: 0.3 g; Sugar: 1.6 g

Zesty Shrimp Cocktail

Preparation Time: 10 minutes
Cooking Time: 1 hour and 15 minutes
Servings: 6

Ingredients:

- 12 ounces smoked shrimp, peeled, deveined
- 1-pound tomatoes
- Two jalapeno pepper, diced
- One small red onion, peeled, sliced 1/4 inch thick
- Three garlic cloves, peeled, halved
- 1 tbsp. olive oil
- 2 tbsp. apple wine vinegar
- 1 ½ teaspoon salt
- 2 tbsp. brown sugar
- 1/4 cup Tabasco sauce
- 1/2 lemon, juiced
- 3 tbsp. cilantro, chopped
- One small avocado, peeled, pitted, flesh cut into 1/2-inch cubes
- 1 ¼ tsp. salt

Directions:

1. Open the smoker's hopper, add dry pallets, make sure ash-can is in place, and then open the ash damper, power on the smoker, and close the ash damper.
2. Set the temperature of the smoker to 350 degrees F, switch smoker to open flame cooking mode, press the open flame 3, remove the grill grates and the batch, replace batch with direct flame insert, then return grates on the grill in the lower position and let preheat for 30 minutes or until the green light on the dial blinks that indicate smoker has reached to set temperature.
3. Then place tomatoes on a rimmed baking sheet, put it on the smoker grill, shut with lid, and smoke for 30 to 45 minutes or until tender and blackened.
4. Meanwhile, take another rimmed baking sheet, add onion and garlic drizzle with oil, and toss until mixed.
5. Place the baking sheet containing onion and garlic on the smoker grill and roast for 15 minutes or until nicely browned, set aside until required.
6. When tomatoes are done, let them rest for 5 minutes, remove their blackened skin, place tomatoes in a food processor, pulse for several times or chopped into small pieces, and then tip tomatoes in a bowl and set aside.
7. Add onion and garlic into the food processor and continue blending until coarsely chopped.
8. Tip onion and garlic mixture in a large bowl, add tomatoes and salt, sugar, vinegar, lemon juice, and hot sauce, and stir until well mixed.
9. Add shrimps and remaining ingredients, stir until combined, and serve.

Nutrition: Calories: 234; Total Fat: 12 g; Saturated Fat: 2 g; Protein: 24 g; Carbs: 7 g; Fiber: 4 g; Sugar: 1 g

Bacon-Wrapped Shrimp

Preparation Time: 10 minutes
Cooking Time: 41 minutes
Servings: 4

Ingredients:

- 16 jumbo shrimp, peeled, deveined
- Eight bacon strips
- ½ tablespoon minced garlic
- 1/4 cup melted butter
- ½ teaspoon ground black pepper
- ¾ teaspoon salt
- 1 tsp. lemon juice

Directions:

1. Open the smoker's hopper, add dry pallets, make sure ash-can is in place, and then open the ash damper, power on the smoker, and close the ash damper.
2. Set the temperature of the smoker to 450 degrees F, switch smoker to open flame cooking mode, press the open flame 3, remove the grill grates and the batch, replace batch with direct flame insert, then return grates on the grill in the lower position and let preheat for 30 minutes or until the green light on the dial blinks that indicate smoker has reached to set temperature.
3. Meanwhile, prepare the shrimps and for this, cut each strip of bacon into half and then wraps each shrimp with bacon strips, securing with a toothpick.
4. Place melted butter in a bowl, add garlic, salt, black pepper, and lemon juice, stir until well mixed and then brush the mixture generously on both sides of the wrapped shrimps.
5. Place shrimps on the smoker grill, shut with lid, and smoke for 11 minutes or until done.
6. When done, transfer shrimps to a dish and serve straight away.

Nutrition: Calories: 182.3; Total Fat: **8.8** g; Saturated Fat: 0.7 g; Protein: 23 g; Carbs: 1 g; Fiber: 0 g; Sugar: 0 g

Smoked Scallops with Citrus and Garlic Butter Sauce

Preparation Time: 10 minutes
Cooking Time: 1 hour and 40 minutes
Servings: 4

Ingredients:

- 2 pounds large scallops
- ½ teaspoon minced garlic
- 2 tsp. salt
- 1/2 small orange zest
- 1 tsp. Ground black pepper
- 1/4 teaspoon Worcestershire sauce
- 8 tbsp. butter, salted, melted
- 1/2 small orange juice
- 1 1/2 teaspoon chopped parsley

Directions:

1. Open the smoker's hopper, add dry pallets, make sure ash-can is in place, and then open the ash damper, power on the smoker, and close the ash damper.
2. Set the smoker's temperature to 225 degrees F, let preheat for 30 minutes or until the green light on the dial blinks that indicate the smoker has reached to set temperature.
3. Meanwhile, rinse scallops, pat dry, and then season with salt and black pepper.
4. Take a baking sheet, place a wire rack on it, arrange seasoned scallops on it, place the baking sheet on the smoker grill, shut the smoker with a lid, and smoke scallops for 20 minutes.
5. Then remove the baking sheet containing scallops from the smoker and set aside until required.
6. Set the temperature of the smoker to 400 degrees F, switch smoker to open flame cooking mode, press the open flame 3, remove the grill grates and the batch, replace batch with direct flame insert, then return grates on the grill in the lower position and let preheat for 30 minutes or until the green light on the dial blinks that indicate smoker has reached to set temperature.
7. Return the baking sheet with scallops on the grill grate, shut with lid, and continue smoking the scallops for 15 minutes or until opaque and tender.
8. Meanwhile, place a saucepan over medium-low heat, add butter and when it melts, add garlic, parsley, and orange zest along with Worcestershire sauce and orange juice, stir until mixed.
9. Boil the sauce for 5 minutes, then remove the saucepan from the heat and keep it warm.
10. When done, transfer scallops to a dish and serve with prepared butter sauce.

Nutrition: Calories: 184; Total Fat: 9 g; Saturated Fat: 5 g; Protein: 21 g; Carbs: 1 g; Fiber: 0 g; Sugar: 0 g

VEGETARIAN RECIPES

Vegan Smoked Carrot Dogs

Preparation Time: 25 minutes
Cooking Time: 35 minutes
Servings: 4

Ingredients:

- 4 thick carrots
- 2 tbsp. avocado oil
- 1 tbsp. liquid smoke
- 1/2 tbsp. garlic powder
- Salt and pepper to taste

Directions:

1. Preheat the Blackstone grill to 425°F and line a baking sheet with parchment paper.
2. Peel the carrots and round the edges.
3. In a mixing bowl, mix oil, liquid smoke, garlic, salt, and pepper. Place the carrots on the baking dish then pour the mixture over.
4. Roll the carrots to coat evenly with the mixture and use fingertips to massage the mixture into the carrots.
5. Place in the grill and grill for 35 minutes or until the carrots are fork-tender ensuring to turn and brush the carrots every 5 minutes with the marinade.
6. Remove from the grill and place the carrots in hot dog bun. Serve with your favorite toppings and enjoy.

Nutrition: Calories: 149 Total Fat: 1.6g Saturated Fat: 0.3g Total Carbs: 27.9g Net Carbs: 24.3g Protein: 5.4g Sugar: 5.6g Fiber: 3.6g Sodium: 516mg Potassium: 60mg

Blackstone grill Smoked Vegetables

Preparation Time: 5 minutes
Cooking Time: 15 minutes
Servings: 6
Ingredients:

- 1 ear corn, fresh, husks and silk strands removed
- 1 yellow squash, sliced
- 1 red onion, cut into wedges
- 1 green pepper, cut into strips
- 1 red pepper, cut into strips
- 1 yellow pepper, cut into strips
- 1 cup mushrooms, halved
- 2 tbsp. oil
- 2 tbsp. chicken seasoning

Directions:

1. Soak the pecan Blackstone in water for an hour. Remove the Blackstones from water and fill the smoker box with the wet Blackstones.
2. Place the smoker box under the grill and close the lid. Heat the grill on high heat for 10 minutes or until smoke starts coming out from the wood chips.
3. Meanwhile, toss the veggies in oil and seasonings then transfer them into a grill basket.
4. Grill for 10 minutes while turning occasionally. Serve and enjoy.

Nutrition: Calories: 97 Total Fat: 5g Saturated Fat: 2g Total Carbs: 11g Net Carbs: 8g Protein: 2g Sugar: 1g Fiber: 3g Sodium: 251mg Potassium: 171mg

Blackstone Grill Spicy Sweet Potatoes

Preparation Time: 10 minutes
Cooking Time: 35 minutes
Servings: 6
   Ingredients:

- 2 lb. sweet potatoes, cut into chunks
- 1 red onion, chopped
- 2 tbsp. oil
- 2 tbsp. orange juice
- 1 tbsp. roasted cinnamon
- 1 tbsp. salt
- 1/4 tbsp. Chipotle chili pepper

Directions:

1. Preheat the Blackstone grill to 425°F with the lid closed.
2. Toss the sweet potatoes with onion, oil, and juice.
3. In a mixing bowl, mix cinnamon, salt, and pepper then sprinkle the mixture over the sweet potatoes.
4. Spread the potatoes on a lined baking dish in a single layer.
5. Place the baking dish in the grill and grill for 30 minutes or until the sweet potatoes are tender.
6. Serve and enjoy.

Nutrition: Calories: 145 Total Fat: 5g Saturated Fat: 0g Total Carbs: 23g Net Carbs: 19g Protein: 2g Sugar: 3g Fiber: 4g Sodium: 428mg Potassium: 230mg

Blackstone Grilled Mexican Street Corn

Preparation Time: 5 minutes
Cooking Time: 25 minutes
Servings: 6
Ingredients:

- 6 ears of corn on the cob
- 1 tbsp. olive oil
- Kosher salt and pepper to taste
- 1/4 cup mayo
- 1/4 cup sour cream
- 1 tbsp. garlic paste
- 1/2 tbsp. chili powder
- Pinch of ground red pepper
- 1/2 cup coria cheese, crumbled
- 1/4 cup cilantro, chopped
- 6 lime wedges

Directions:

1. Brush the corn with oil.
2. Sprinkle with salt.
3. Place the corn on a Blackstone grill set at 350°F. Cook for 25 minutes as you turn itoccasionally.
4. Meanwhile mix mayo, cream, garlic, chili, and red pepper until well combined.
5. Let it rest for some minutes then brush with the mayo mixture.
6. Sprinkle cottage cheese, more chili powder, and cilantro. Serve with lime wedges. Enjoy.

Nutrition: Calories: 144 Total Fat: 5g Saturated Fat: 2g Total Carbs: 10g Net Carbs: 10g Protein: 0g Sugar: 0g Fiber: 0g Sodium: 136mg Potassium: 173mg

Smoked Broccoli

Preparation Time: 10 minutes
Cooking Time: 30 minutes
Servings: 4
Ingredients:

- 2 heads broccoli
- Kosher salt
- 2 tablespoons vegetable oil
- Fresh Pepper (ground)

Directions:

1. Preheat your smoker to 350F.
2. Separate the florets from the heads.
3. Coat the broccoli with vegetable oil by tossing. Thereafter, season with salt and pepper.
4. Using a grilling basket, put the broccoli on the grate of the smoker and smoke for 30 minutes or till crisp.
5. Enjoy!

Nutrition: Calories- 76| Fat- 7g| Saturated fat- 1.3g| Protein- 1.3g| Carbohydrates- 3.1g|

Smoked Mushrooms 2

Preparation Time: 10 minutes
Cooking Time: 1 hour
Servings: 4
Ingredients:

- 2 lb. mushrooms (Button or Portabella)
- 2 cups Italian dressing
- Pepper
- Salt

Directions:

1. In a gallon zip lock bag, add in the mushrooms.
2. Pour in the Italian dressing in the zip lock bag and some pepper and salt to taste.
3. Refrigerate for 1 hour.
4. Once ready to cook, preheat your smoker to 250F.
5. Smoke mushrooms for an hour or till much soft and a bit smaller in size.
6. Note: mushrooms will smoke well at any temperature so long as they don't burn.

Nutrition: Calories- 392| Fat- 34g| Saturated fat- 5.3g| Carbohydrates- 19.8g| Fiber- 2.3g| Sugar- 13.7g| Protein- 7.6g| Cholesterol- 79mg| Sodium- 196mg|

Smoked Butternut Squash

Preparation Time: 15 minutes

Cooking Time: 1 hour 30 minutes

Servings: 5

Ingredients

- 1 whole butternut squash
- 2 tablespoons olive oil
- 1 tablespoon brown sugar
- 1/2 tablespoon chili powder
- 1 teaspoon black pepper
- 1 teaspoon kosher salt
- 1/2 teaspoon garlic powder

Directions:

1. Preheat your smoker to 325F.
2. Half the squash lengthwise with a knife. Make lines to its flesh as shown above.
3. In a bowl, add the olive oil, garlic pepper, chili powder and brown sugar and combine. Brush this mixture on the expose top part.
4. Put the butternut squash on the smoker and smoke for 1.5 hours or till your preferred tenderness. Brush the squash with the mixture once more on the last 30 minutes of smoking.
5. Remove from the smoker.

Nutrition: Calories- 11O| Fat- 5.9g| Saturated fat- 0.8g| Carbohydrates- 15.7g| Protein- 1.3g| Sodium- 478mg| Cholesterol- 0mg|

Smoke-Grilled Eggplant

Preparation Time: 10 minutes
Cooking Time: 10 minutes
Servings: 4
Ingredients:

- 1 eggplant (large in size)
- 4 tablespoons coconut aminos
- 2 tablespoons avocado oil
- 2 teaspoons cumin (ground)
- 2 teaspoons smoked paprika
- 2 teaspoons coriander (ground)
- 2 teaspoons cumin (ground)
- 1/2 teaspoon cayenne pepper
- 1/2 teaspoon garlic powder
- 1/2 teaspoon sea salt

Directions:

1. Cut the eggplant lengthwise to 1/4-inch slices. Drizzle and brush the eggplant slices with the coconut aminos and avocado oil.
2. In a small mixing bowl, combine the spices. Sprinkle the mix on the slices on both sides, ensuring they are full coated.
3. Preheat your grill to medium high heat and place the slices. Grill each side for 3 minutes till they become tender.
4. Remove from the grill and enjoy.

Nutrition: Calories- 62| Fat- 1.5g| Saturated fat- 0.2g| Carbohydrates- 11.6g| Protein- 1.6g| Calcium- 23mg| Potassium- 337mg| Iron- 1mg|

Smoked Vegetables

Preparation Time: 15 minutes
Cooking Time: 45 minutes
Servings: 4
  Ingredients:

- Summer squash (sliced)
- Olive oil
- Balsamic vinegar
- Red onion
- Zucchini (sliced)
- Red pepper
- Black pepper
- Garlic (sliced)
- Sea salt

Directions:

1. Add all ingredients in a mixing bowl and combine.
2. Preheat smoker to 350F.
3. Smoked for 30 to 45 minutes or till well cooked through.

Nutrition: Calories- 120| Fat- 7g| Sat fat- 1g| Carbohydrates- 12g| Protein- 2g| Potassium- 514mg| Sodium- 595mg| Fiber- 2g| Sugar- 7g| Vitamin C- 67.3mg| Vitamin A- 1225IU|

VEGAN RECIPES

Beef Jerky

Preparation Time: 15 minutes
Cooking Time: 4 hours
Servings: 6
Ingredients:

THE MEAT

- Beef roast – 2 pounds

THE MARINADE

- Jalapeno peppers, cored and sliced – 2
- Onion powder – 1 teaspoon
- Garlic powder – 1 teaspoon
- Salt – 1 tablespoon
- Ground black pepper – 2 teaspoons
- Dr. Pepper – 2 cups
- Worcestershire sauce – 1 tablespoon

Directions:

1. Before setting smoker, marinade beef.
2. For this, slice beef thinly against the grain and place in a large plastic bag.
3. Place all the ingredients for marinade in a saucepan, stir until combined and bring to boil.
4. Then reduce heat to low and let simmer for 15 minutes or more until sauce is reduced by half.
5. Then remove the pan from heat and let cool completely.
6. Add this cooled marinade to the beef, seal the bag and turn upside down until well coated.
7. Place this bag in the refrigerator and let beef marinade for 12 hours.
8. Then remove beef slices from marinade, pat dry using paper towels and place on jerky or cooling rack.
9. When ready to smoke, place a prepared pouch of woodchips over charcoal and when smoke starts, place jerky rack on the smoker.
10. Set lid on smoker and monitor temperature through temperature gauge or temperature probes and maintain it.

RED MEAT RECIPES

Smoked Lamb Leg

Preparation Time: 10 minutes
Cooking Time: 4 hours
Servings: 4-6
Ingredients:

The Meat

- 1 Lamb leg.

The Mixture

- Honey – ¼ cup.
- Sierra Dijon Mustard – 2 tbsp.
- Chopped rosemary – 2 tbsp.
- Lemon zest – 1 tsp.
- Garlic (minced) – 3 cloves.
- Ground black pepper – 1 tsp.

The Fire

- Wood pellet smoker.

Directions:

1. It is better to have frozen piece of lamb leg. So, you can shave off as much fat as you like.
2. Mix garlic, lemon zest, chopped rosemary, mustard, pepper, and honey in a bowl. Put a saran wrap and place the leg of lamb on top of it. Pour the mixture on top of it.
3. Alternatively, you can use zip lock bag for this process Wrap the lamb leg up and put it in the refrigerator.
4. Let it sit in the fridge overnight. Take the wrap off the meat or take it out of zip lock bag if you have used it.
5. Take 3-4 garlic cloves and insert it in the meat. Sprinkle over the meat some seasonings, which include salt, pepper, and cayenne. Slow smoking is the method of cooking used for the lamb meat in this recipe.
6. Set the temperature at 200 and watch your meat thermometer probe. When it reaches 130 degrees take it out and let it rest for 20 minutes.
7. Make ¼ inch standards cut for serving meat and pour the juices on top of it to serve.

Nutrition: Energy (calories): 413 kcal Protein: 51.28 g Fat: 13.55 g Carbohydrates: 19.99 g

BAKING RECIPES

Bacon, Egg, And Cheese Sandwich

Preparation Time: 15 minutes
Cooking Time: 20 minutes
Servings: 4

Ingredients

- 2 large eggs
- 2 tablespoons of milk or water
- A pinch of salt to taste
- A pinch of pepper to taste
- 3 teaspoons of butter
- 4 slices of white bread
- 2 slices of Jack cheese
- 4 slices of bacon

Directions:

1. Using a small mixing bowl, add in the eggs, milk, salt, and pepper to taste then mix properly to combine.
2. Preheat a Blackstone Smoker and Grill to 400 degrees F for about ten to fifteen minuteswith its lid closed.
3. Place the bacon slices on the preheated grill and grill for about eight to ten minutes, flipping once until it becomes crispy. Set the bacon aside on a paper-lined towel.
4. Decrease the temperature of the grill to 350 degrees F, place a grill pan on the grill, and let it heat for about ten minutes.
5. Spread two tablespoons of butter on the cut side of the bread, place the bread on the skillet pan and toast for about two minutes until brown in color.
6. Place the cheese on the toasted bread, close the lid of the grill then cook for about one minute until the cheese melts completely, set aside. Still using the same grill pan, add in the rest of the butter then let melt. Pour in the egg mixture and cook for a few minutes until it is cooked as desired.
7. Assemble the sandwich as desired then serve.

Nutrition: Calories 401 cal Fat 23g Carbohydrates 26g Fiber 3g Protein 23g

CHEESE AND BREAD

Smoked Salted Caramel Apple Pie

Preparation Time: 30 minutes
Cooking Time: 30 minutes
Servings: 4-6
Ingredients:

For the apple pie:

- One pastry (for double-crust pie)
- 6 Apples
- For the smoked, salted caramel:
- 1 cup brown sugar
- ¾ cup light corn syrup
- 6 tbsp. butter (unsalted, cut in pieces)
- 1 cup warm smoked cream
- 1 tsp. sea salt

Directions:

Grill Prep:

1. Fill a container with water and ice
2. Grab a shallow, smaller pan, and then put in your cream. Take that smaller pan and place it in the large pan with ice and water.
3. Set this on your wood pellet smoker grill for 15 to 20 minutes.
4. For the caramel, mix your corn syrup and sugar in a saucepan, and then cook it all using medium heat. Be sure to stir every so often until the back of your spoon is coated and begins to turn copper.
5. Next, add the butter, salt, and smoked cream, and then stir.
6. Get your pie crust, apples, and salted caramel. Put a pie crust on a pie plate, and then fill it with slices of apples.
7. Pour on the caramel next.
8. Put on the top crust over all of that, and then crimp both crusts together to keep them locked in.
9. Create a few slits in the top crust so that the steam can be released as you bake.
10. Brush with some cream or egg, and then sprinkle with some sea salt and raw sugar.

On the Grill:

1. Set up your wood pellet smoker grill for indirect cooking.
2. Preheat your wood pellet smoker grill for 10 to 15 minutes at 375 degrees Fahrenheit, keeping the lid closed as soon as the fire gets started (should take 4 to 5 minutes, tops).
3. Set the pie on your grill, and then bake for 20 minutes.

4. At the 20-minute mark, lower the heat to 325 degrees Fahrenheit, and then let it cook for 35 minutes more. You want the crust to be a nice golden brown, and the filling should be bubbly when it's ready.
5. Take the pie off the grill and allow it to cool and rest.
6. Serve with some vanilla ice cream and enjoy!

Nutrition: Calories: 149 Cal Fat: 2 g Carbohydrates: 30 g Protein: 3 g Fiber: 2 g

APPETIZERS AND SIDES

Cheesy Sausage Balls

Preparation time: 15 minutes
Cooking time: 30 minutes
Servings 4 to 5
Ingredients:

- 1 pound (454 g) ground hot sausage, uncooked
- 8 ounces (227 g) cream cheese, softened
- 1 package mini filo dough shells

Directions:

1. Supply your smoker with wood pellets and follow the manufacturer's specific start-up procedure. Preheat, with the lid closed, to 350°F (177°C).
2. In a large bowl, using your hands, thoroughly mix together the sausage and cream cheese until well blended.
3. Place the filo dough shells on a rimmed perforated pizza pan or into a mini muffin tin.
4. Roll the sausage and cheese mixture into 1-inch balls and place into the filo shells.
5. Place the pizza pan or mini muffin tin on the grill, close the lid, and smoke the sausage balls for 30 minutes, or until cooked through and the sausage is no longer pink.
6. Plate and serve warm.

Nutrition: Calories: 57 Total Fat: 3 g Saturated Fat: 1 g Total Carbs: 6 g Net Carbs: 4 g Protein: 4 g Sugars: 2 g Fiber: 2 g Sodium: 484 mg

Corn and Crab Cakes

Preparation time: 25 minutes
Cooking time: 10 minutes
Servings 30 mini crab cakes

Ingredients

- Nonstick cooking spray, oil, or butter, for greasing
- 1 cup panko bread crumbs, divided
- 1 cup canned corn, drained
- ½ cup chopped scallions, divided
- ½ red bell pepper, finely chopped
- 16 ounces (454 g) jumbo lump crab meat
- ¾ cup mayonnaise, divided
- 1 egg, beaten
- 1 teaspoon salt
- 1 teaspoon freshly ground black pepper
- 2 teaspoons cayenne pepper, divided
- Juice of 1 lemon

Directions:

1. Supply your smoker with wood pellets and follow the manufacturer's specific start-up procedure. Preheat, with the lid closed, to 425°F (218°C).
2. Spray three 12-cup mini muffin pans with cooking spray and divide ½ cup of the panko between 30 of the muffin cups, pressing into the bottoms and up the sides. (Work in batches, if necessary, depending on the number of pans you have.)
3. In a medium bowl, combine the corn, ¼ cup of scallions, the bell pepper, crab meat, half of the mayonnaise, the egg, salt, pepper, and 1 teaspoon of cayenne pepper.
4. Gently fold in the remaining ½ cup of bread crumbs and divide the mixture between the prepared mini muffin cups.
5. Place the pans on the grill grate, close the lid, and smoke for 10 minutes, or until golden brown.
6. In a small bowl, combine the lemon juice and the remaining mayonnaise, scallions, and cayenne pepper to make a sauce.
7. Brush the tops of the mini crab cakes with the sauce and serve hot.

Nutrition: Calories: 57 Total Fat: 3 g Saturated Fat: 1 g Total Carbs: 6 g Net Carbs: 4 g Protein: 4 g Sugars: 2 g Fiber: 2 g Sodium: 484 mg

MORE SIDES

Queso Chorizo Meal

Preparation Time: 10-15 minutes
Cooking Time: 60 minutes
Servings: 4
Ingredients

- 16 ounces cubed Velveeta cheese
- 4 ounces cream cheese, cubed
- 10 ounces Rotel
- 1 pound cooked Chorizo, chopped
- How To
- Take your drip pan and add water, cover with aluminum foil. Pre-heat your smoker to 200 degrees F
- Use water fill water pan halfway through and place it over drip pan. Add wood chips to the side tray
- Add all of the ingredients in an aluminum foil pan and smoke for 1 hour, stirring after every 15 minutes
- Serve with tortilla chips
- Enjoy!

Nutrition: Calories: 372 Fat: 30g Carbohydrates: 6g Protein: 6g

Spectacular Smoked Peach

Preparation Time: 20 minutes
Cooking Time: 35-45 minutes
Servings: 4

Ingredients

- tablespoons honey
- 1-pint vanilla ice cream
- 1 tablespoon packed brown sugar
- 4 barely ripe peaches, halved and 3 pitted

Directions:

1. Take your drip pan and add water, cover with aluminum foil. Pre-heat your smoker to 200 degrees F
2. Use water fill water pan halfway through and place it over drip pan. Add wood chips to the side tray
3. Sprinkle cut peach halves with brown sugar
4. Transfer prepared peach to smoker and smoke for 30-45 minutes
5. Drizzle honey and serve
6. Enjoy!

Nutrition: Calories: 309 Fats: 27g Carbs: 17g Fiber: 2g

A Meaty Bologna

Preparation Time: 20 minutes
Cooking Time:60 minutes
Serving: 6-8
Ingredients

- Salt and pepper to taste
- ¼ cup yellow mustard
- 5 pounds all-beef bologna chub
- 1 teaspoon garlic powder
- 1 teaspoon ground nutmeg
- 1 teaspoon ground coriander
- 2 tablespoons packed brown sugar
- 2 tablespoons chili powder

Directions:

1. Take your drip pan and add water, cover with aluminum foil. Pre-heat your smoker to 250 degrees F
2. Use water fill water pan halfway through and place it over drip pan. Add wood chips to the side tray
3. Take a small-sized bowl and add chili powder, coriander, nutmeg, brown sugar, garlic
4. Mix well and keep it on the side
5. Cut bologna into ½ inch slices, making sure that there are few small cuts all around the edges
6. Coat them generously with mustard mix
7. Season generously with salt and pepper, spice mix
8. Transfer to Smoker and smoke for 1 hour
9. Serve and enjoy once done!

Nutrition: Calories: 819 Fats: 46g Carbs: 1g Fiber: 2g

Simple Dump Cake

Preparation Time: 20 minutes
Cook Time: 60 – 120 minutes
Serving: 6-8

Ingredients

- 1 box cake mix of your choosing
- 2 cans of your desired pie filling
- 1 stick of butter

Directions:

1. Take your drip pan and add water, cover with aluminum foil. Pre-heat your smoker to 250 degrees F
2. Use water fill water pan halfway through and place it over drip pan. Add wood chips to the side tray
3. Spread the contents of the pie to the bottom of a container, sprinkle cake mixes on top
4. Melt butter in a saucepot and drizzle over cake mix
5. Transfer to the smoker and bake for about 60-120 minutes
6. Enjoy!

Nutrition: Calories: 328 Fat: 9g Carbohydrates: 61g Protein: 2g

SNACKS

For Maggi Macaroni and Cheese

Preparation Time: 30 mins.
Cooking Time: 1 hr. 30 mins.
Servings: 8

Ingredients:

- ¼ c. all-purpose flour
- ½ stick butter
- Butter, for greasing
- One-pound cooked elbow macaroni
- One c. grated Parmesan
- 8 ounces cream cheese
- Two c. shredded Monterey Jack
- 3 t. garlic powder
- Two t. salt
- One t. pepper
- Two c. shredded Cheddar, divided
- 3 c. milk

Directions:

1. Put the butter into the pot and melt. Mix in the flour. Stir constantly for a minute. Mix in the pepper, salt, garlic powder, and milk. Let it boil.
2. After lowering the heat, let it simmer for about 5 mins, or until it has thickened. Remove from the heat.
3. Mix in the cream cheese, parmesan, Monterey jack, and 1 ½ c. of cheddar. Stir everything until melted. Fold in the pasta.
4. Add wood pellets to your smoker and follow your cooker's startup procedure. Preheat your smoker, with your lid closed, until it reaches 225.
5. Butter a 9" x 13" baking pan. Pour the macaroni mixture to the pan and lay on the grill. Cover and allow it to smoke for an hour, or until it has become bubbly. Top the macaroni with rest of the cheddar during the last
6. Serve.

Nutrition: Calories: 493 Protein: 19.29g Carbs: 52.15g Fat: 22.84g

DESSERT RECIPE

Fast S'Mores Dip Skillet

Preparation time: 5 minutes
Total cooking time: 6-8 minutes
Servings: 4-6
Ingredients:

- 2 tbsp. salted butter, melted
- ¼ cup milk
- 12 ounces (340 g) semisweet chocolate chips
- 16 ounces (454 g) Jet-Puffed marshmallows
- Graham crackers and apple wedges, for serving

Directions:

1. Supply your smoker with wood pellets and follow the manufacturer's specific start-up procedure. Preheat, with the lid closed, to 450°F (232°C).
2. Place a cast-iron skillet on the preheated grill grate and pour in the melted butter and milk, stirring for about 1 minute.
3. Once the mixture starts to heat, top with the chocolate chips in an even layer and arrange the marshmallows standing up to cover all of the chocolate.
4. Close the lid and smoke for 5 to 7 minutes, or until the marshmallows are lightly toasted.
5. Remove from the heat and serve immediately with graham crackers and apple wedges for dipping.

Nutrition: Energy (calories): 893 kcal Protein: 7.1 g Fat: 42.02 g Carbohydrates: 143.07 g

Blackberry Pie

Preparation time: 15 minutes
Total cooking time: 20-25 minutes
Servings: 4-6

Ingredients:

- Nonstick cooking spray or butter, for greasing
- One box (2 sheets) refrigerated piecrusts
- 8 tbsp. (1 stick) unsalted butter, melted, plus eight tablespoons (1 stick) cut into pieces
- ½ cup all-purpose flour
- 2 cups sugar, divided
- 2 pints blackberries
- ½ cup milk
- Vanilla ice cream, for serving

Directions:

1. Supply your smoker with wood pellets and follow the manufacturer's specific start-up procedure. Preheat, with the lid closed, to 375degrees F (191°C).
2. Coat a cast-iron skillet with cooking spray.
3. Unroll one refrigerated piecrust and place it in the bottom and up the side of the skillet. Using a fork, poke holes in the crust in several places.
4. Set the skillet on the grill grate, close the lid, and smoke for 5 minutes, or until lightly browned. Remove from the grill and set aside.
5. In a large bowl, combine the stick of melted butter with the flour and 1½ cups of sugar.
6. Add the blackberries to the flour-sugar mixture and toss until well coated.
7. Spread the berry mixture evenly in the skillet and sprinkle the milk on top. Scatter half of the cut pieces of butter randomly over the mixture.
8. Unroll the remaining piecrust, place it over the top of the skillet, slice the dough into even strips, and weave it into a lattice. Scatter the remaining pieces of butter along the top of the crust.
9. Sprinkle the remaining ½ cup of sugar on top of the crust and return the skillet to the smoker.
10. Close the lid and smoke for 15 to 20 minutes, or until bubbly and brown on top. It may be necessary to use some aluminum foil around the edges near the end of the cooking time to prevent the crust from burning.
11. Serve the pie hot with some vanilla ice cream.

Nutrition: Energy (calories): 295 kcal Protein: 2.83 g Fat: 11.41 g Carbohydrates: 46.8 g

Frosted Carrot Cake

Preparation time: 20 minutes
Total cooking time: 60 minutes
Servings: 4-6
Ingredients:

- Eight carrots, peeled and grated
- Four eggs, at room temperature
- 1 cup of vegetable oil
- ½ cup milk
- 1 tsp. vanilla extract
- 2 cups of sugar
- 2 cups self-rising or cake flour
- 2 tsp. baking soda
- 1 tsp. salt
- 1 cup finely chopped pecans
- Nonstick cooking spray or butter, for greasing
- 8 ounces (227 g) cream cheese
- 1 cup confectioners' sugar
- 8 tbsp. (1 stick) unsalted butter, at room temperature
- 1 tsp. vanilla extract
- ½ teaspoon salt
- 2 tbsp. to ¼ cup milk

Directions:

For the Cake

1. Supply your smoker with wood pellets and follow the manufacturer's specific start-up procedure. Preheat, with the lid closed, to 350°F (177°C).
2. In a prepared blender, combine the grated carrots, eggs, oil, milk, vanilla, and process until the carrots are finely minced.
3. In a large mixing bowl, combine the sugar, flour, baking soda, and salt.
4. Add the carrot mixture to the flour mixture and stir until well incorporated. Fold in the chopped pecans.
5. Glaze a 9-by-13-inch baking pan with cooking spray.
6. Spill the batter into the prepared pan and place on the grill grate. Close the lid and smoke for about 1 hour, or until a toothpick inserted in the center comes out clean.
7. Remove the cake from the grill and let cool completely.

For the Frosting

8. Using an electric mixer on low speed, beat the cream cheese, confectioners, sugar, butter, vanilla, and salt, adding two tablespoons to ¼ cup of milk to thin the frosting as needed.
9. Frost the cooled cake and slice to serve.

Nutrition: Energy (calories): 1116 kcal Protein: 13.37 g Fat: 75.47 g Carbohydrates: 102.02 g

Lemony Smokin' Bars

Preparation time: 30 minutes
Total cooking time: 60 minutes
Servings: 8-12

Ingredients:

- ¾ cup lemon juice
- 1½ cup sugar
- Two eggs
- Three egg yolk
- 1½ teaspoon cornstarch
- Pinch sea salt
- 4 tbsp. unsalted butter
- ¼ cup olive oil
- ½ tablespoon lemon zest
- 1¼ cup flour
- ¼ cup granulated sugar
- Three tablespoon confectioner's sugar
- 1 tsp. lemon zest
- ¼ teaspoon sea salt, fine
- 10 tbsp. unsalted butter, cut into cubes

Directions:

1. When you're ready to cook, set grill temperature to 180°F (82°C) and preheat, lid closed for 15 minutes.
2. In a prepared small bowl, combine the lemon juice, sugar, eggs and yolks, cornstarch and acceptable sea salt. Pour into a baking sheet or cake pan and place on the grill. Smoke for 30 minutes, whisking the mixture halfway through cooking. Take from grill and set aside.
3. Pour mixture into a small saucepan. Place on a stovetop set to medium heat until boiling. Once boiling, boil for 60 seconds. Take from heat and strain through a mesh strainer into a bowl. Whisk in cold butter, olive oil, and lemon zest.
4. To make a crust, whisk together the flour, granulated sugar, powdered sugar, lemon zest, and salt in a food processor. Add the butter and blend until you get a crumbly dough. Press the dough into a prepared 9 "by 9" baking sheet lined with parchment paper that is long enough to hang on 2 of the sides. When ready to cook, set the pellet grill to 350°F (177°C) and preheat, lid closed for 15 minutes.
5. Bake or cook until crust is very lightly golden brown, about 30 to 35 minutes.
6. Remove from the grill and pour the lemon filling over the crust. Return to grill and continue to bake until filling is just set, about 15 to 20 minutes.
7. Allow to cool at room temperature, then refrigerate until chilled before slicing into bars. Sprinkle with confectioners' sugar and flaky sea salt right before serving. Enjoy!

Nutrition: Energy (calories): 246 kcal Protein: 2.91 g Fat: 14.85 g Carbohydrates: 26.05 g

Chocolate Chip Brownie Pie

Preparation time: 20 minutes
Total cooking time: 45 minutes
Servings: 8-12
Ingredients:

- ¾ cup lemon juice
- 1½ cup sugar
- Two eggs
- Three egg yolk
- 1½ teaspoon cornstarch
- Pinch sea salt
- 4 tbsp. unsalted butter
- ¼ cup olive oil
- ½ tablespoon lemon zest
- 1¼ cup flour
- ¼ cup granulated sugar
- Three tablespoon confectioner's sugar
- 1 tsp. lemon zest
- ¼ teaspoon sea salt, fine
- 10 tbsp. unsalted butter, cut into cubes

Directions:

1. When ready to cook, set grill temperature to 180°F (82°C) and preheat, lid closed for 15 minutes.
2. In a small mixing bowl, whisk together lemon juice, sugar, eggs and yolks, cornstarch, and acceptable sea salt. Pour into a sheet tray or cake pan and place on the grill. Smoke for 30 minutes, whisking mixture halfway through smoking. Remove from grill and set aside.
3. Pour mixture into a small saucepan. Place on a stovetop set to medium heat until boiling. Once boiling, boil for 60 seconds. Remove from heat and strain through a mesh strainer into a bowl. Whisk in cold butter, olive oil, and lemon zest.
4. To make a crust, pulse together the flour, granulated sugar, confectioners 'sugar, lemon zest, and salt in a food processor. Add butter and pulse until just mixed into a crumbly dough. Press dough into a prepared 9" by 9" baking dish lined with parchment paper that is long enough to hang over 2 of the sides.
5. When ready to cook, turn the temperature to 350°F (177°C) and preheat, lid closed for 15 minutes.
6. Bake until crust is very lightly golden brown, about 30 to 35 minutes.
7. Remove from the grill and pour the lemon filling over the crust. Return to grill and continue to bake until filling is just set, about 15 to 20 minutes.
8. Allow to cool at room temperature, then refrigerate until chilled before slicing into bars. Sprinkle with confectioners' sugar and flaky sea salt right before serving. Enjoy!

Nutrition: Energy (calories): 368 kcal Protein: 4.37 g Fat: 22.27 g Carbohydrates: 39.08 g

Bourbon Maple Pumpkin Pie

Preparation time: 20 minutes
Total cooking time: 45 minutes
Servings: 8-12•

Ingredients:

- ½ cup semisweet chocolate chips
- 1 cup butter
- 1 cup brown sugar
- 1 cup of sugar
- Four whole eggs
- 2 tsp. vanilla extract
- 2 cup all-purpose flour
- 2/3 cup cocoa powder, unsweetened
- 1 tsp. baking soda
- 1 tsp. salt
- 1 cup semisweet chocolate chips
- ¾ cup white chocolate chips
- ¾ cup nuts (optional)
- 1 (8-ounce / 227-g) whole hot fudge sauce
- Two tablespoon Guinness beer

Directions:

1. Coat the inside of a 10-inch pie plate with non-stick cooking spray.
2. When ready to cook, set the grill temperature to 350°F (177°C) and preheat, lid closed for 15 minutes.
3. Melt ½ cup (100 g) of the semi-sweet chocolate chips in the microwave—cream together butter, brown sugar, and granulated sugar. Beat in the eggs, adding one at a time and mixing after each egg, and the vanilla. Add in the melted chocolate chips.
4. On a large piece of wax paper, sift together the cocoa powder, flour, baking soda, and salt. Lift the corners of the form and pour slowly into the butter mixture.
5. Beat until the dry ingredients are just incorporated. Stir in the remaining semi-sweet chocolate chips, white chocolate chips, and nuts. Press the dough into the prepared pie pan.
6. Place the brownie pie on the grill and bake for 45-50 minutes or until the pastry is set in the middle. Rotate the pan halfway through cooking. If the top or edges begin to brown, cover the top with a piece of aluminum foil.
7. In a microwave-safe measuring cup, heat the fudge sauce in the microwave. Stir in the Guinness.
8. Once the brownie pie is done, allow sitting for 20 minutes. Slice into wedges and top with the fudge sauce. Enjoy.

Nutrition: Energy (calories): 838 kcal Protein: 9.23 g Fat: 49.83 g Carbohydrates: 99.74 g

SAUCES AND RUBS

Avocado Salsa

Preparation Time: 10 Minutes
Cooking Time: 30 Minutes
Servings: 4
Ingredients:

- 2 avocados
- 1 onion
- 1 jalapeno
- 2 garlic cloves
- ¼ cup red wine vinegar
- 1 tablespoon lime juice
- ¼ cup parsley leaves

Directions:

1. In a blender place all ingredients and blend until smooth
2. Pour smoothie in a glass and serve

Nutrition: Calories: 60 Carbs: 13g Fat: 1g Protein: 0g

Barbeque Sauce

Preparation Time: 10 Minutes
Cooking Time: 30 Minutes
Servings: 4

Ingredients:

- ¼ cup ketchup
- 1 tablespoon brown sugar
- 1 tsp molasses
- 1 tsp hot sauce
- 1 tsp mustard
- 1 tsp onion powder

Directions:

1. In a blender place all ingredients and blend until smooth
2. Pour smoothie in a glass and serve

Nutrition: Calories: 60 Carbs: 13g Fat: 1g Protein: 0g

NUT AND FRUIT RECIPES

Chocolate Chip Cookies

Preparation Time: 30 minutes
Cooking Time: 30 minutes
Servings: 12
Ingredients:

- 1 ½ cup chopped walnuts
- One teaspoon vanilla
- Two cup chocolate chips
- One teaspoon baking soda
- 2 ½ cups plain flour
- ½ teaspoon salt
- 1 ½ stick softened butter
- Two eggs
- One cup brown sugar
- ½ cup sugar

Directions:

1. Add Blackstones to your smoker and follow your cooker's startup procedure. Preheat
   your smoker, with your lid closed, until it reaches 350.
2. Mix together the baking soda, salt, and flour.
3. Cream the brown sugar, sugar, and butter. Mix in the vanilla and eggs until it comes together.
4. Slowly add in the flour while continuing to beat. Once all flour has been incorporated, add in the chocolate chips and walnuts. Using a spoon, fold into batter.
5. Place an aluminum foil onto grill. In an aluminum foil, drop spoonfuls of dough and bake for 17 minutes.

Nutrition: Calories: 66.5 cal Protein: 1.8g Fiber: 0g Carbohydrates: 5.9g Fat: 4.6g

Caramel Bananas

Preparation Time: 15 minutes
Cooking Time: 15 minutes
Servings: 4

Ingredients:

- 1/3 cup chopped pecans
- ½ cup sweetened condensed milk
- 4 slightly green bananas
- ½ cup brown sugar
- 2 tablespoon corn syrup
- ½ cup butter

Directions:

1. Add Blackstone to your smoker and follow your cooker's startup procedure. Preheat your smoker, with the lid closed, until it reaches 350.
2. Place the milk, corn syrup, butter, and brown sugar into a heavy saucepan and bring to boil. For five minutes, simmer the mixture in low heat. Stir frequently.
3. Place the bananas with their peels on, on the grill and let them grill for five minutes. Flip and cook for five minutes more. Peels will be dark and might split.
4. Place on serving platter. Cut the ends off the bananas and split peel down the middle. Take the peel off the bananas and spoon caramel on top. Sprinkle with pecans.

Nutrition: Calories: 345 cal Protein: 11g Fiber: 3.1g Carbohydrates: 77g Fat: 1g

Simple Apple Pie

Preparation Time: 30 minutes
Cooking Time: 50 minutes
Servings: 8
Ingredients:

- One frozen pie crust, thawed
- ¼ cup sugar
- ¼ cup peach preserves
- 1 tablespoon cornstarch
- 5 apples, cored, sliced thin

Directions:

1. Add Blackstone to your smoker and follow your cooker's startup procedure. Preheat your
   smoker, with the lid closed, until it reaches 375.
2. Mix the cornstarch, sugar, and apples together. Set to the side.
3. Unroll the pie crust and put into a pie pan. Spread the peach preserves evenly on the crust. Lay the apples out onto the crust. Fold the crust over apples.
4. Place on baking sheet upside down on the grill. Place the pie pan on top and bake for 35 minutes. Cool for five minutes before slicing.

Nutrition: Calories: 320 cal Protein: 2g Carbohydrates: 47g Fiber: 5g Fat: 15g

TRADITIONAL RECIPES

Halibut Delight

Preparation Time: 4-6 hours
Cooking Time: 15 minutes
Servings: 4-6
Ingredients:

- ½ a cup of salt
- ½ a cup of brown sugar
- 1 teaspoon of smoked paprika
- 1 teaspoon of ground cumin
- 2 pound of halibut
- 1/3 cup of mayonnaise

Directions:

1. Take a small bowl and add salt, brown sugar, cumin, and paprika
2. Coat the halibut well and cover, refrigerate for 4-6 hours
3. Take your drip pan and add water, cover with aluminum foil. Pre-heat your smoker to 200 degrees F
4. Use water fill water pan halfway through and place it over drip pan. Add wood chips to the side tray
5. Remove the fish from refrigerator and rinse it well, pat it dry
6. Rub the mayonnaise on the fish
7. Transfer the halibut to smoker and smoke for 2 hours until the internal temperature reaches 120 degrees Fahrenheit

Nutrition: Calories: 375 Fats: 21g Carbs: 10g Fiber: 2g

Roast Rack of Lamb

Preparation Time: 10 minutes
Cooking Time: 1 hour
Servings: 6-8
Ingredients:

- Blackstone Flavor: Alder
- 1 (2-pound) rack of lamb
- 1 batch Rosemary-Garlic Lamb Seasoning

Directions:

1. Supply your smoker with Blackstones and follow the manufacturer's specific start-upprocedure. Preheat the grill to 450°F.
2. Using a boning knife, score the bottom fat portion of the rib meat.
3. Using your hands, rub the rack of lamb with the lamb seasoning, making sure it penetrates into the scored fat.
4. Place the rack directly on the grill grate and smoke until its internal temperature reaches 145F.
5. Take off the rack from the grill and let it rest for 20 to 30 minutes, before slicing into individual ribs to serve.

Nutrition: Calories: 50 Carbs: 4g Fiber: 2g Fat: 2.5g Protein: 2g

Ultimate Lamb Burgers

Preparation Time: 20 minutes
Cooking Time: 30 minutes
Servings: 4
Ingredients:

Blackstones:
AppleBurger:

- 2 lbs. ground lamb
- 1 jalapeño
- 6 scallions, diced
- 2 tablespoons mint
- 2 tablespoons dill, minced
- 3 cloves garlic, minced
- Salt and pepper
- 4 brioche buns
- 4 slices manchego cheese

Sauce:

- 1 cup mayonnaise
- 2 teaspoons lemon juice
- 2 cloves garlic
- 1 bell pepper, diced
- salt and pepper

Directions

1. When ready to cook, turn your smoker to 400F and preheat.
2. Add the mint, scallions, salt, garlic, dill, jalapeño, lamb, and pepper to the mixing bowl.
3. Form the lamb mixture into eight patties.
4. Lay the pepper on the grill and cook for 20 minutes.
5. Take the pepper from the grill and place it in a bag, and seal. After ten minutes, remove pepper from the bag, remove seeds and peel the skin.
6. Add the garlic, lemon juice, mayo, roasted red pepper, salt, and pepper and process until smooth. Serve alongside the burger.
7. Lay the lamb burgers on the grill, and cook for five minutes per side, then place in the buns with a slice of cheese, and serve with the homemade sauce.

Nutrition: Calories: 50 Carbs: 4g Fiber: 2g Fat: 2.5g Protein: 2g

Citrus- Smoked Trout

Preparation Time: 10 minutes

Cooking Time: 1 to 2 hours

Servings: 6 to 8

Ingredients:

- 6 to 8 skin-on rainbow trout, cleaned and scaled
- 1-gallon orange juice
- ½ cup packed light brown sugar
- ¼ cup salt
- 1 tablespoon freshly ground black pepper
- Nonstick spray, oil, or butter, for greasing
- 1 tablespoon chopped fresh parsley
- 1 lemon, sliced

Directions:

1. Fillet the fish and pat dry with paper towels
2. Pour the orange juice into a large container with a lid and stir in the brown sugar, salt, and pepper
3. Place the trout in the brine, cover, and refrigerate for 1 hour
4. Cover the grill grate with heavy-duty aluminum foil. Poke holes in the foil and spray with cooking spray
5. Supply your smoker with Blackstones and follow the manufacturer's specific start-upprocedure. Preheat, with the lid closed, to 225°F
6. Remove the trout from the brine and pat dry. Arrange the fish on the foil-covered grill grate, close the lid, and smoke for 1 hour 30 minutes to 2 hours, or until flaky
7. Remove the fish from the heat. Serve garnished with the fresh parsley and lemon slices.

Nutrition: Calories: 220, Protein: 33 g Fat: 4 g, Carbohydrates: 17 g,

Sunday Supper Salmon with Olive Tapenade

Preparation Time: 1 hour and 20 minutes

Cooking Time: 1 to 2 hours

Servings: 10 to 12

Ingredients:

- 2 cups packed light brown sugar
- ½ cup salt
- ¼ cup maple syrup
- ⅓ cup crab boil seasoning
- 1 (3- to 5-pound) whole salmon fillet, skin removed
- ¼ cup extra-virgin olive oil
- 1 (15-ounce) can pitted green olives, drained
- 1 (15-ounce) can pitted black olives, drained
- 3 tablespoons jarred sun-dried tomatoes, drained
- 3 tablespoons chopped fresh basil
- 1 tablespoon dried oregano
- 2 tablespoons freshly squeezed lemon juice
- 2 tablespoons jarred capers, drained
- 2 tablespoons chopped fresh parsley, plus more for sprinkling

Directions:

1. In a medium bowl, combine the brown sugar, salt, maple syrup, and crab boil seasoning.
2. Rub the paste all over the salmon and place the fish in a shallow dish. Cover and marinate in the refrigerator for at least 8 hours or overnight.
3. Remove the salmon from dish, rinse, and pat dry, and let stand for 1 hour to take off the chill.
4. Meanwhile, in a food processor, pulse the olive oil, green olives, black olives, sun-dried tomatoes, basil, oregano, lemon juice, capers, and parsley to a chunky consistency. Refrigerate the tapenade until ready to serve.
5. Supply your smoker with Blackstones and follow the manufacturer's specific start-upprocedure. Preheat, with the lid closed, to 250°F.
6. Place the salmon on the grill grate (or on a cedar plank on the grill grate), close the lid, and smoke for 1 to 2 hours, or until the internal temperature reaches 140°F to 145°F. When the fish flakes easily with a fork, it's done.
7. Remove the salmon from the heat and sprinkle with parsley. Serve with the olive tapenade.

Nutrition: Calories: 240; Proteins: 23g; Carbs: 3g; Fat: 16g

Grilled Tuna

Preparation Time: 20 minutes
Cooking Time: 4 hours
Servings: 6
Ingredients:

- Albacore tuna fillets – 6, each about 8 ounces
- Salt – 1 cup
- Brown sugar – 1 cup
- Orange, zested – 1
- Lemon, zested – 1

Directions:

1. Before preheating the grill, brine the tuna, and for this, prepare brine stirring together all of its ingredients until mixed.
2. Take a large container, layer tuna fillets in it, covering each fillet with it, and then let them sit in the refrigerator for 6 hours.
3. Then remove tuna fillets from the brine, rinse well, pat dry and cool in the refrigerator for 30 minutes.
4. When the grill has preheated, place tuna fillets on the grilling rack and let smoke for 3 hours, turning halfway.
5. Check the fire after one hour of smoking and add more wood pallets if required.
6. Then switch temperature of the grill to 225 degrees F and continue grilling for another 1 hour until tuna has turned nicely golden and fork-tender.
7. Serve immediately.

Nutrition: Calories: 311; Fiber: 3 g; Saturated Fat: 1.2 g; Protein: 45 g; Carbs: 11 g; Total Fat: 8.8 g; Sugar: 1.3 g

Grilled Swordfish

Preparation Time: 10 minutes
Cooking Time: 18 minutes
Servings: 4
Ingredients:

- Swordfish fillets – 4
- Salt – 1 tablespoon
- Ground black pepper – ¾ tablespoon
- Olive oil – 2 tablespoons
- Ears of corn – 4
- Cherry tomatoes – 1 pint
- Cilantro, chopped – 1/3 cup
- Medium red onion, peeled, diced – 1
- Serrano pepper, minced – 1
- Lime, juiced – 1
- Salt – ½ teaspoon
- Ground black pepper – ¼ teaspoon

Directions:

1. In the meantime, prepare fillets and for this, brush them with oil and then season with salt and black pepper.
2. Prepare the corn, and for this, brush with olive oil and season with ¼ teaspoon each of salt and black pepper.
3. When the grill has preheated, place fillets on the grilling rack along with corns and grill corn for 15 minutes until light brown and fillets for 18 minutes until fork tender.
4. When corn has grilled, cut kernels from it, place them into a medium bowl, add remaining ingredients for the salsa and stir until mixed.
5. When fillets have grilled, divide them evenly among plates, top with corn salsa and then serve.

Nutrition: Calories: 311; Total Fat: 8.8 g; Saturated Fat: 1.2 g; Fiber: 3 g; Protein: 45 g; Sugar: 1.3 g Carbs: 11 g;

Lamb Kebabs

Preparation Time: 15 minutes
Cooking Time: 10 minutes
Servings: 4
   Ingredients:

Blackstones: Mesquite

- 1/2 tablespoon salt
- 2 tablespoons fresh mint
- 3 lbs. leg of lamb
- 1/2 cup lemon juice
- 1 tablespoon lemon zest
- 15 apricots, pitted
- 1/2 tablespoon cilantro
- 2 teaspoons black pepper
- 1/2 cup olive oil
- 1 teaspoon cumin
- 2 red onion

Directions:

1. Combine the olive oil, pepper, lemon juice, mint, salt, lemon zest, cumin, and cilantro. Add lamb leg, then place in the refrigerator overnight.
2. Remove the lamb from the marinade, cube them, and then thread onto the skewer with the apricots and onions.
3. When ready to cook, turn your smoker to 400F and preheat.
4. Lay the skewers on the grill and cook for ten minutes.
5. Remove from the grill and serve.

Nutrition: Calories: 50 Carbs: 4g Fiber: 2g Fat: 2.5g Protein: 2g

SAUCES, RUBS, AND MARINATES

Smoked Turkey Legs Rub

Preparation Time: 5 minutes
Cooking Time: 0 minutes
Servings: 1
Ingredients:

- 3 tbsp. Onion powder
- 2 tbsp. Paprika
- 1 tbsp. Garlic powder
- 1 tsp. ground Pepper
- 1 tsp. ground Cumin
- 3 tbsp. Vegetable oil

Directions:

1. Simply place all ingredients into an airtight jar, stir well to combine then close.
2. Use within six months.

Nutrition: Calories: 10 Sugar: 1g Protein: 2g

Smoked Cajun Chicken Rub

Preparation Time: 5 minutes
Cooking Time: 5 minutes
Servings: 1

Ingredients:

- 2 tbsp. Onion powder
- 1 tsp. dried Oregano
- 2 tbsp. Cayenne pepper
- 2 tsp. Paprika
- 2 tsp. Garlic powder
- 6 tbsp. Louisiana-style hot Marinade
- 2 tsp. Lawry's seasoning salt
- 1 tsp. Black pepper
- 1 tsp. dried thyme

Directions:

1. Simply place all ingredients into an airtight jar, stir well to combine then close.
2. Use within six months.

Nutrition: Calories: 5 Carbs: 1g

Fennel & Almonds Sauce

Preparation Time: 10 minutes
Cooking Time: 30 minutes
Servings: 4

Ingredients

- 1 cup fennel bulb
- 1 cup olive oil
- 1 cup almonds
- 1 cup fennel fronds

Directions

1. Place all those available ingredients in a blender and blend those.
2. Now the smoothie is ready to pour into a glass and serve

Nutrition: Energy (calories): 504 kcal Protein: 1.06 g Fat: 54.31 g Carbohydrates: 5.92 g

Sauce Thai Dipping

Preparation Time: 10 minutes
Cooking Time: 30 minutes
Servings: 4

Ingredients:

- 6 tsp. garlic sauce
- 2 tbsp. fish sauce
- 2 tbsp. lime juice
- 1 tbsp. brown sugar
- 1 tsp. chili flakes

Directions

1. On your blender, place all ingredients and blend until smooth
2. Now the smoothie is ready to pour into a glass and serve

Nutrition: Energy (calories): 14 kcal Protein: 1.16 g Fat: 0.21 g Carbohydrates: 2.6 g

Chili Dipping Sauce

Preparation Time: 10 minutes
Cooking Time: 30 minutes
Servings: 4
Ingredients

- 1 tsp. chili
- Two garlic cloves
- ¼ cup brown sugar
- 2 tbsp. red wine vinegar

Directions

1. On your blender, place all ingredients and blend until smooth
2. Now the smoothie is ready to pour into a glass and serve

Nutrition: Energy (calories): 57 kcal Protein: 0.16 g Fat: 0.1 g Carbohydrates: 14.09 g

RUBS, INJECTABLES, MARINADES, AND MOPS

<u>Worcestershire Mop and Spritz</u>

Preparation Time: 10 Minutes
Cooking Time: 0 Minutes
Servings: 1 Cup
Ingredients:

- ½ cup water
- ½ cup Worcestershire sauce
- 2 garlic cloves, sliced

Directions:

1. In a small bowl, stir together the water, Worcestershire sauce, and garlic until mixed. Transfer to a spray bottle for spritzing. Refrigerate any unused spritz for up to 3 days and use for all kinds of meats.

Nutrition: Calories: 20 Carbs: 9g Protein: 5g

OTHER RECIPES YOU NEVER THOUGHT ABOUT TO GRILL

Mghinese five-spice powder

Preparation Time: 10 minutes
Cooking Time: 3 hours and 30 minutes
Servings: 6
Ingredients:

- 3 lb. pork shoulder, sliced into cubes
- 2 tablespoons pulled dry pork rub
- 1 cup chicken broth
- 2 tablespoons olive oil
- Corn tortillas
- 3 jalapeno pepper, minced
- Cilantro, chopped
- Fresh cheese, crumbled
- Red onion, sliced

Directions:

1. Turn on your wood pellet grill.
2. Set it to 300 degrees F.
3. Sprinkle the pork cubes with the dry rub.
4. Place in a Dutch oven.
5. Pour in the chicken broth.
6. Add the Dutch oven on top of the grill.
7. Open the sear slide.
8. Bring to a boil.
9. Cover the Dutch oven and seal the sear slide.
10. Simmer for 2 hours and 30 minutes.
11. Uncover and open the sear slide.
12. Bring to a boil.
13. Take the Dutch oven off the grill. Set aside.
14. Pour the olive oil into a pan over medium heat.
15. Fry the pork for 10 minutes.
16. Top the corn tortillas with the pork cubes and the rest of the ingredients.

Tip: You can also smoke the pork cubes before braising.
Nutrition: Calories: 501 Protein: 44g Vitamin D: 5mcg 26% Calcium: 122mg 9% Iron: 16mg: 90% Potassium: 625mg

Roasted Korean Short Ribs

Preparation Time: 15 minutes
Cooking Time: 9 hours
Servings: 4
Ingredients:

- 1 cup beef stock
- 1/2 cup soy sauce
- 3 cloves garlic, peeled
- 1 tablespoon ginger, minced
- 1-tablespoon beef and brisket dry rub
- 2 tablespoons brown sugar
- 1-tablespoon hot sauce
- 4 beef short ribs

Directions:

1. In a bowl, put all the ingredients and mix it, except the short ribs.
2. Add the ribs to a baking pan.
3. Pour the mixture on top of the ribs.
4. Cover and marinate in the refrigerator for 4 hours.
5. Set your wood pellet grill to 250 degrees F.
6. Roast the ribs for 4 hours.
7. Serving Suggestion: Garnish with sesame seeds and chopped green onion. Serve with Kimchi.

Nutrition: Calories: 641 Protein: 0.7g Vitamin D: 0mcg

Roasted Rosemary Lamb

Preparation Time: 10 minutes
Cooking Time: 4 hours
Servings: 2
Ingredients:

- 1 lamb rack
- 2 rosemary sprigs, chopped
- Salt and pepper to taste
- 12 baby potatoes
- 1/2 cup butter
- 1 bunch asparagus
- 2 tablespoons olive oil

Directions:

1. Set your wood pellet grill to 225 degrees F.
2. Sprinkle the lamb with the rosemary, salt, and pepper.
3. In a baking pan, add the potatoes and coat with the butter.
4. Add the lamb to the grill.
5. Place the pan with potatoes beside the lamb.
6. Roast for 3 hours.
7. Coat the asparagus with the olive oil.
8. For the last 20 minutes, mix the asparagus into the potatoes.
9. Serve the lamb with the asparagus and baby potatoes.

Nutrition: Calories: 321 Total Carbohydrate 15.5g 6% Dietary Fiber: 0.3g 1% Total Sugars 13.5g Protein: 42.2g

CONCLUSION

In conclusion, it is a fact that the Blackstone pellet grill has made grilling easier and better for humanity, and Grilling, which is part of the so-called "dietetic" cooking, had been made easier through the Blackstone grill. Giving us that tasty meal, we've been craving for and thus improving the quality of life. This book made you a lot of recipes that you can make at your home with your new Blackstone Pellet grill. The recipes will give so much satisfaction with the tenderness and tasty BBQ.

The Blackstone barbecues are electrical, and a typical 3-position function controls them. A cylindrical device transmits the pellets from the storage to the fire place, like a pellet stove. Blackstone Grill smoker promotes an excellent outcome for your meat and other recipes. This smoker provides a tasty for your foods. To achieve such a real taste, you need the quality of materials and get the exact smoking. It is best if you get the maximum consistency of smoking so that you can have the best result of your meat and other recipes. Moreover, if you add more flavors to your recipes, use the best wood pellet for cooking for your food.

Many people ask me questions on why I chose Blackstone pellet grill, and you might think, well, the answer is clear and true, and yes! It's right before us. Why?

It cooks with a wood fire, giving an excellent quality in taste because nothing is like it: real wood, real smoking, natural aroma. In terms of the cooking process, it has changed a lot. Experts chefs tend to have new experiments with new flavor and ingredients to create a delicious and tasty recipe.

Grilling is one of the most popular cooking processes that grant a perfect taste to your recipes. Grilling is a much healthier method than others because its benefits food, preserves flavor, and nutrients. But from the other side, a Blackstone grill smoker's wood pellet grill allows you to grill your food quickly and with less effort and smoke. The advantage of having a Blackstone grill smoker in your home is the versatility, helps you cook food faster, provides a monitoring scale for the temperature,and it is one of the essential parts of cooking.

It is a versatile barbecue. In fact, it can be grilled, smoked, baked, roasted, and stewed—everything you can imagine cooking with the Blackstone grill smoker. You will find that this Blackstone grill smoker is aflexible tool that has a good service.

As we all could testify that using the pellet grill has been made simple by Blackstone: its intuitive control panel has a power button and a knobthat allows you to adjust the temperature comfortably.

Finally, we need to note that through Grilling, we can always find new flavors in our dishes: with Blackstone pellets, you can smoke your dishes, giving them an ever new and different flavor. Blackstone Grill smoker isthe answer you are looking for your taste buds. Don't waste your time and have your own smoker at home and start cooking your favorite recipes with this book.

Lightning Source UK Ltd.
Milton Keynes UK
UKHW021843170621
385713UK00002B/319